Korean Culture for Curious New Comers

Korean Culture for Curious New Comers

Textcopyright © 2009 by Hannah Park
Photocopyrights © 2009 by Culture Heritage Administration of Korea *et al.*

Published by Pagijong press
129-162 Yongdu-dong, Dongdaemun-gu,
Seoul, Korea
Tel : 82-2-922-1192
Fax : 82-2-928-4683
www.pjbook.com
Printed in Seoul, Korea
ISBN 978-89-6292-725-2 03300

Korean Culture for Curious New Comers

Author Hannah Park · Translator Chong-Hoon Chun

Pagijong Press

To Satisfy Foreigners Curious About Korean Culture

Visitors to Korea often ask questions, "Where can I find a good place for shopping?" "I find the Korean flag very beautiful. Could you tell me the meaning of it?"

Some who live in Korea or those who are here learning the Korean language are often embarrassed by Koreans asking "How old are you?" at their first meeting, and cannot understand how Koreans share *jige*, a dish similar to western stew, from a common bowl without using individual plates.

To the former, a simple booklet introducing Korea would do. But for the latter, the explanation is not that easy.

There are hundreds of thousands of foreigners living in Korea. Some are here for study, some for work and some live here with their Korean husbands. There are, however, only a few books available that may satisfactorily give answers to such curiosity. The author kept this in mind before starting this book - to attend to foreigners living the Korean life with cultural shocks.

The author, having lived several years in China, also had many questions about the way the Chinese people live, such as 'why do Chinese people are fond of rich or greasy food?' Nevertheless, I could not find a book that satisfied my curiosity. Likewise, I thought, foreigners living in Korea must have questions regarding the way the Korean people live, the way the Koreans think, etc. Why do Koreans take their shoes off in restaurants, they would ask, which is only natural to Koreans. This book, therefore, explains things that are seen rather unusual from foreigners' view point but go by unquestioned to the Korean natives.

What is customary to and taken for granted by Koreans is the very culture unique to Korea. Such uniqueness becomes vivid when seen in comparison with other cultures outside Korea. Such uniqueness becomes understandable to foreigners when given in a comparative way with other cultures. For example, the meaning of '*jimjilbang*' can be better explained to foreigners if they are given chances to understand the Korean ondol system, heated floor. Furthermore, so doing, they would come to understand that it also helps their blood circulation and would enjoy '*jimjilbang*'.

I spent 10 years in China since 1999, when China had the vision, "China, The Next Generation." I taught the Korean language and the culture at several colleges and universities there, when few teaching material on Korean culture was available. Only a few PR brochures put out by the Korean government were available. Whenever I had chance for a visit to Korea, I scraped whatever material that I thought would help my teaching back in China, including the Seoul metro map and newspaper ads. That being still insufficient, I had to improvise a book 'an outlook of Korea' to aid my lectures, which was well acclaimed by the Chinese students. It is this book, with years of collection and compilation, that motivated me to write this book.

Such questionnaires I asked to the students each semester for several years as 'what comes in your mind when think of Korea,' 'what do you want to know about Korea most,' together with reports, magazines and newspapers published in China were used to make up for the lacking reference materials. Also, writings on Korea by foreigners who had lived a long time in Korean were referred to.

Added to that were my personal experiences and perception from living abroad. Generally speaking, an academic approach is essential to understand a culture, of course, but understanding of it by living the culture should not be underestimated.

My experiences from living in China provided me with a valuable opportunity to understand uniqueness of Korean culture most distinctly. Had I lived in the U.S., I would not have pondered over the difference between kimchi and pickle as the two are obviously different. In China, however, as there are many salty food similar to kimchi, I had to give more thought trying to understand the real difference between the two including their origins. Thanks to my living abroad, my thought on foreigners is no longer fixed. I can understand why each country has different educational system, and this understanding even allows me to think freely of blending some parts of the difference with the Korean system for good outcome.

In this book, 'nature' and 'person' are employed as the two main role players of culture to describe the Korean society. Largely, it is the nature that affects the living culture as it provides essential necessities, while it is the people that lead spiritual culture with variants of language and history. Once you have the clue, the rest comes along easily. With this book, the readers would find it easy to adapt themselves to Korean culture. Once they have come to understand the essence of Korean culture, learning the Korean language becomes so much easier.

I am confident that this book will be a guiding light to foreigners and the members of multi-cultural families in understanding the Korean society. Nothing would please me more if my readers find a better way to adapt themselves to the Korean lifestyle with help of this book. I also sincerely hope that the teachers of Korean culture would benefit from this book as well as children of compatriots abroad in understanding more about their mother country.

My heartfelt gratitude goes to Mr. Pak Chan-ik who gladly accepted publication of this book, Ms. Lee Young-hee, the editor-in-chief and her colleagues at the publishing company, Professor Hwang of the Korean Culture Institute at central University of Nationalities of China, and professors in Korea and China who have been lavish in encouragement for harvest of this book, my dear 80-year-old mother who is an ardent fan of mine, and finally to the one who is in heaven.

On a hot summer day in 2009,

Hannah Park

The Korean Language Society has spent 100 years elaborating on Korean language. Recently, as the educators of Korean language have been actively interacting with each other overseas, Korean language plays a greater role in globalization. Especially with the rise of multiculturalism in Korean society, the Korean Language Society, the most renowned academic society in Korea, is researching on the materials of Korean society and culture and working on spreading the use of Korean language.

This is why the publication of "Korean Culture for Curious New Comers" is especially pleasing.

I have been hearing about this book for several years. Every time I visited China regarding Korean language tests, I noticed how the number of Korean language conferences has been increasing. That is when I first encountered the first draft written by the author of this book who was writing it while teaching "Korean Language as a Foreign Language and Korean Culture" in China, and I encouraged her that this book would turn out to be a great book with the author's keen insight into Korean culture. Since then, it has been 3 years, and now the book is about to be published. Given that it takes a lot less time to publish books with the development of publishing technology nowadays, a long period of time has been spent on this book before finally being published. Surely, the author must have been spending that much time pointing out every aspect of Korean culture that foreigners are curious about and comparing Korean culture with foreign cultures.

Upon opening the pages of the book, I can imagine how much effort the author has put in the book. This book introduces Korea as a whole including clothes, food, houses, sports and trips with a main focus on natural environment and socio-cultural variations to enable readers easily understand Korea in general. As well structured as the book is, the content is not stiff, and it is in relation with everyday life to make it easily comprehensible. For example, in chapter 2 where the author relates Korea having fresh water in nature with having many beautiful women and in chapter 4 where the habit of Koreans passing a liquor glass around the table is explained as a way of expressing intimacy, arisen from sacrificial drink at ancestral rites, such elaborations are very interesting and convincing. In fact, through the author's keen observation, I learned a lot about our own customs and cultures I haven't reflected on before even as a Korean myself. I got more interested in our culture as I got to go abroad on business trips regarding Korean Language Association. Once, a foreigner asked me "Why do Koreans dip their spoons in the same pot when they eat stew?" I believe I am not the only one who has heard of such questions outside of Korea.

As can be seen from the table of contents, this book comprises almost all the fields of Korean society and briefly yet clearly explains how Korean cultures of today are formed in relation with history. At the same time, the author's efforts to emphasize on what foreigners would like to know about can be found on every page. It is hard for us to perceive ourselves objectively; however, the author observes and gains an insight into our culture from outside of Korea and clarifies it for readers. In short, "Korean Culture for Curious New Comers" is a book greatly introducing Korean cultures, which Hannah Park has been researching and teaching for years, at foreigners' level. I am confident that this book will be very useful in aiding foreign college students and multicultural families to understand and adapt to Korean cultures in a short period of time.

By all means, I wish readers can use this book to grasp an idea about Korean society. I am sure this book will function as a vivid primer on Korea. I hope to share this book especially with Korean language teachers abroad. It will help us deeply reflect on various customs and cultures we just take for granted even as we live within the culture. I recommend this book as it is worth reading for everyone more than anything.

President of the Korean Language Society,
Seung-gon Kim

contents

contents

Vibrant South Korea, Dynamic Korea!

Step 1 South Korea in the World

The official name of South Korea is the Republic of Korea. In the Korean language, South Korea is referred to as han guk 한국, the abbreviation for '*dae han min guk* 대한민국.' South Korea is a peninsula state which lies at the eastern end of the Asian continent and which is located at 33 and 34 degrees north latitude and 124 and 131 degrees east longitude. The Korean peninsula is bordered by China and Russia to the north and it is separated from Japan to the south by the Korea Strait.

Korea, China and Japan are geographically close. It takes one hour or more to fly west over the Yellow Sea from Korea to China and east across the East Sea from Korea to Japan. Korea share the same time zone with Japan. But, the local time in Korea is earlier than in China. When Westerners find a Korean, they often ask the Korean whether he or she is 'Chinese' or 'Japanese.' This is because people in the three countries look very similar and Asians coming from a cultural sphere of Chinese characters.

Korea played a role in accepting, recreating and conveying culture because of its geographical feature such as lying between China and Japan. Korea reinvented Chinese culture into Korean culture to cultivate its creative ones acknowledged as a World Heritage Site. Further, Korea gave them to Japan, acting as a bridge between Chinese and Japanese cultures.

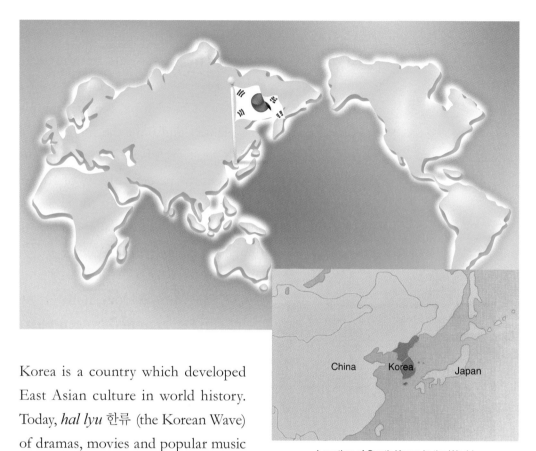

Location of South Korea in the World
Locations of Korea, China and Japan

Korea is a country which developed East Asian culture in world history. Today, *hal lyu* 한류 (the Korean Wave) of dramas, movies and popular music sweeps across Asia. The basis of the wave is formed by Korea's distinctive culture created in the long history of the Korean Peninsula. So, the followings are reborn as the brand 'Korean Wave' and compose a new 'space for culture' enjoyed by citizens all over the world including Asia: hangeul 한글 (the Korean alphabet), *tae geuk* 태극 (Great Absolute), *han bok* 한복 (traditional Korean dress), kimchi 김치 (Korean pickled vegetables), *bul go gi* 불고기 (Korean broiled meat), taekwondo 태권도 (one of Korean martial arts), *go ryeo in sam* 고려인삼 (Korean ginseng), arirang 아리랑 (the representative korean song), and *tal chum* 탈춤 (Korean mask dance-dramas).

Korea was invaded frequently by its neighboring countries because it has been located on a peninsula for a long time. In the history of hardships, Korean people solidified their ethnic identity and built the high level of moral culture uniting themselves. There were two events praised by foreign presses in the modern history of Korea: gold collection campaign and advancement to the semi-finals at the 2012 FIFA World Cup in Korea and Japan. First of all, the campaign enabled Korean people to get through the financial crisis in a short of period of time after Korea received $57 billion in bailout money from IMF in 1997. Then, Korean people showed their persistence and passion again by cheering for their soccer team during the World Cup games. Their strong will was formed by the wisdom coming from continuous invasions of other countries. So, Korea is a country which bounces back up like a roly poly.

Korea has a history of five thousand years and a long-developed culture. In contrary, Korea is not large in land size. The Korean peninsula is two hundred twenty thousand square kilometers. The land area of it is almost equal to that of the United Kingdom and Italy. If the two Koreas were to reunite, their total population would reach about seventy million. The capital city of Korea is 'Seoul.' Over ten million people live in the city. *nam dae mun* 남대문 (The Great South Gate), originally called *sung nye mun* 숭례문, was the main entrance to Han yang 한양 (now Seoul), the capital of the Joseon Dynasty. Because products all over the country were gathered in the gate, Namdaemun Market has been one of Korea's representative shopping meccas for a long time. As Korea's National Treasure No. 1. the Great South Gate is a high pride of Korean people as well as citizens of Seoul. Korea is the only divided country in the world. In 1953, after the Korean War, the boundary between the two Koreas South Korea and North Korea was fixed in the form of demilitarized zone (DMZ). South Korea amazed the world by achieving an economic revival called the 'Miracle of the Han River' 30 years after the war. Further, South Korea grew and developed to be the host of the 1988 Olympic Games. There were building breaks down because of poor construction caused by its rapid economic growth. As the Korean national character is expressed as 'Chop-chop!', Korean people's hot temper is criticized.

Now, the gross national income (GNI) per capita of South Korea has exceeded twenty thousand dollars. South Korea is the 14th largest economy in the world. On October 13, 2006, Ki-Moon Ban was elected to be the 8th Secretary General by the United Nations General Assembly. As South Korea is increasing its global presence, it is providing development assistance to 130 countries and working for the world peace. In the past, Korea was called 'the Land of the Morning Calm,' But, today, South Korea is known throughout the world for its image 'Dynamic Korea' as it is emerging as the strongest power in the IT world and the Korean Wave is spreading.

1. The Korean flag

The Korean flag (*tae geuk gi* 태극기 in Korean) is the national flag of South Korea.

The national flag was legally established at the end of the Joseon Dynasty in 1883. Waving the Korean flag, Korean people cheered passionately for their soccer team during the 2012 FIFA World Cup in Korea and Japan. This surprised the world. In those days, all of South Korea was filled with the Korean flags. Some people drew the Korean flag on their face. Other people wrapped the Korean flag around them. When foreigners see the Korean flag, they say, 'It's very beautiful!' Or, they ask, 'Do you know what the unique pattern of the Korean flag symbolizes?'

The Korean flag is painted on a white background with black stripes around the central circle. In the four corners are placed trigram *gwe* 괘 in black. The four gwe consists of *geon* 건, *gon* 곤, *gam* 감 and *yi* 리. *Geon* symbolizes heaven; *gon* earth; *gam* water; *yi* fire. The central *tae geuk* pattern symbolizes the theory of yin-yang and the five elements and it is composed of the red upper half circle *yang* 양 and the blue lower half circle *yin* 음.

The *tae geuk* pattern reflecting the *yin-yang* thought of the Orient has

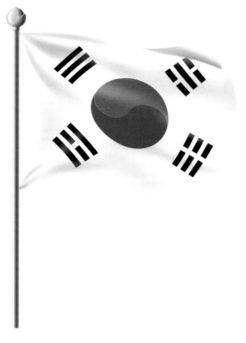

tae geuk gi (The Korean national flag)
Rose of Sharon (The Korean national flower)

been widely used. It can be found in many parts such as
tteok sal 떡살 (rice cake patterns) to stamp designs onto
rice cakes, *bang pae yeon* 방패연 (shield kite), *jang go* 장고
(hourglass drum), *bu cha*e 부채 (fan), pattern of front door,
and corner of palace stairs. Nowadays it is used for various
logos symbolizing Korea. Putting their right hand on their
left breast toward the national flag, Korean people sing the
national anthem at the ceremony of national holiday.

2. The Korean national anthem

Ae guk ga 애국가 is the Korean national anthem.

The Korean national anthem has been sung since it was written one hundred years ago. It has four verses and is in four-four time. It is played relatively slowly under a solemn atmosphere. Contrary to those of other countries, the words of the Korean national anthem do not strengthen ideas such as freedom and equality but describe only nature in its purest form. This shows that Korean people share a national characteristic of loving nature.

3. Rose of Sharon

mu gung hwa 무궁화 (Rose of Sharon) is Korea's national flower.

The Korean name mu gung hwa literally means 'flowers blooming endlessly and forever.' Not only does rose of Sharon stand the coldness well but it also has a tenacious hold on life. This symbolizes ethnicity of Korean people expressed as 'industriousness and patience.' It used as the symbol of public institutions, such as National Assembly or courts, and medals. There are many songs on rose of Sharon. I introduce one of them as follows. Because the lyrics of it is simple and repetitive, it is very useful for Korean learning.

Rose of Sharon

Rose of Sharon, rose of Sharon, Korea's national flower
In the whole land of Korea, Korea's national flower
Bloomed, bloomed, Korea's national flower
In the whole land of Korea, Korea's national flower

4. National and public holidays

- Independence Movement Day (March 1): Celebrates the movement for resistance against Japanese colonial rule on March 1, 1919.
- Constitution Day (July 17): Celebrates the promulgation of the Korean Constitution on July 17, 1948.
- Liberation Day (August 15): Celebrates the end of Japanese colonial rule on August 15, 1945.
- National Foundation Day (October 3): Celebrates Dangun's founding the first Korean kingdom on October 3, 2333 B.C.
- Hangeul Day (October 9): Celebrates that Sejong the Great created

hangeul 한글 (the Korean alphabet).

The above days are national holidays. There are public holidays, such as New Year's Day (January 1), *seol nal* 설날 (Lunar New Year's Day) (January 1 on the lunar calendar), Independence Movement Day (March 1), Buddha's Birthday (April 8 on the lunar calendar), Children's Day (May 5), Memorial Day (June 6), Liberation Day (August 15), Harvest Moon Festival (August 15 on the lunar calendar), National Foundation Day (October 3), and Christmas (December 25). Lunar New Year's Day and Harvest Moon Festival are Korean people's important holidays and allow them to have a three-day long weekend.

5. The Korean Peninsula's indices

- Area: Approx. 220,000 ㎢ (South Korea: Approx. 100,000 ㎢)
- Population: Approx. 74,000,000 (South Korea: Approx. 50,000,000)
- Language: Korean
- Capital: Seoul
- Political system: Democratic republicanism
- Government system: Presidentialism
- Monetary unit: Won
- Gross domestic product (GDP): 1,129,200,000,000 dollars (ranked 14th largest in the world)
- Gross national income (GNI) per capita: 2,270,800,000,000 dollars
- Images: The land of the morning calm, the country of courteous people in the East, and dynamic Korea

* National Statistical Office (NSO), 2012

Step 3　Korean People and the Korean Alphabet

1. Korean people

Korean people are called '*han min jok* 한민족' or '*han gyeo re* 한겨레' in Korean.

The word *han* literally means 'great.' In the Korean Peninsula there were three han confederacies of *ma han* 마한, *jin han* 진한 and *byun han* 변한 in the bronze age. It has been said that han came from the confederacies. Korean people are called '*bae dal gyeo re* 배달겨레' in Korean because they are descendants of King *dan gun* 단군, who established the first Korean kingdom Ancient Joseon. The identity of Korean people was established as one ethnic race when the territory of Korea was set along the two boundaries the Yalu River and the Tumen River in the early years of the Joseon Dynasty.

Korean people have a strong ethnic identity. We can find it from the fact that Korean people overcame hardships with perfect unity when they were invaded by countries. This ethnicity might come from self-defense against invasion. The strong identity means that people of the country adjacent to such large countries as China are aware of crisis situations which can bring them down unless all of them hang together. There are two motive powers of the strong solidarity. The one is Korea's fast information delivery. When the very existence of Korea was at stake, the news was delivered quickly to the people because it was a small country. So, Korean people could unite and fight as if it was one of family affairs whenever Korea was invaded by other country. The other one is that Korean people use one language and the Korean alphabet (hangeul 한글) which is easy to learn. This enabled them to strengthen the characteristic of one race when communicating with one another and exchanging emotions.

Korea was invaded by foreign powers such as the West or Japan after the late 19th century. In those days, Korean people trapped by war and famine moved abroad. They have struggled successfully against a lot of difficulties to build Korean communities in peace and prosperity. They spread out to more than 170 countries, including the United States, China and South American countries and form the so-called Global Korean Community of 7 million overseas Koreans or more. Nowadays there has been an increase in Korean citizens who study or do business abroad. All of overseas Korean residents, regardless of their nationality, are Korea's valuable ethnic assets to keep Korean culture and emotion while living abroad.

These days, there are many foreigners in Korea. More foreigners are working in South Korea thanks to its continuous economic growth. The number of foreigners who married to Korean citizens is growing rapidly in South Korea. The homogeneous ethnic identity was the prime mover in Korean people's defending their country against foreign invasions. But, the 21st century is a time when Korean people should take a prerequisite of mutual coexistence of all the people in the world. Korean people should not take an unfriendly attitude toward foreigners living in South Korea which is one of the negative aspects of the homogeneous ethnic identity. Instead, Korean people should embrace those foreigners. Further, Korean people residing overseas should keep pace with all ethnic groups who try to achieve the common prosperity of people all around the world, while promoting positive aspects of the homogeneous ethnic identity to widen the consciousness to a multicultural society.

2. The Korean alphabet

The Korean alphabet (hangeul 한글) is Korea's unique and remarkable phonetic script.

There are several thousand languages currently spoken, but less than one hundred of them have a writing system. Korean people have the most superior writing system. The *hun min jeong eum* manuscript 훈민정음 해례본 on the writing system was registered as the UNESCO World Documentary Heritage in 1997. They enjoy literacy to live a life of abundance. That is to say, the illiteracy rate is 0% in South Korea.

Korean is the language spoken by more than 80 million Korean people

Typing Korean on a computer is faster and more accurate because in the Korean mode, all the consonants are entered by the left hand and all the vowels are entered by the right hand.

in and outside Korea regardless of nationality. It is the 12th or 14th largest language in the world. The number of Korean learners is expected to rise higher because of Korea's economic strength and the Korean Wave (hal lyu 한류). Today, a lot of studies of the Korean alphabet (hangeul 한글) have been published in linguistic circles of Korea and other countries. Every Hangeul Day (October 9) these studies are introduced by the media in Korea. This shows that South Korea is greatly interested in moral culture.

Superiority of the Korean alphabet

First, the Korean alphabet (hangeul 한글) is the world's only writing system whose origin is clearly known: (1) who invented it, (2) when it was invented and (3) for what purpose it was invented by

The creator of most writing systems and their creation date are not known. In 1443 the Korean alphabet was created by Sejong the Great, and it was promulgated in 1446. In those days, the alphabet was called '*hun min jeong eum* 훈민정음', which means the correct sounds for instructing the people. The name 'hangeul 한글' was introduced by Si-Gyeong Choo in 1928 during the Japanese colonial era.

Before Sejong the Great invented the Korean alphabet, all of Korean people used Chinese characters because they did not have their own written language. The people had trouble in expressing their thoughts in writing hard to learn Chinese characters when they try to talk to about the unjust situation they were in. In the preface of the *hun min jeong eum* manuscript 훈민정음 해례본, Sejong the Great described clearly the purpose of creation of the Korean alphabet as the people's having their own written language easy to learn. In 1989 'the UNESCO King Sejong Prize' was established to honor the outstanding contribution made to literacy by Sejong the Great. The prize is rewarded to governments or governmental agencies and non-governmental organizations (NGOs) achieving particularly effective results in the promotion of literacy.

Second, the Korean alphabet is easy to learn and use.

In the *hun min jeong eum* manuscript, a Korean neo-Confucian scholar In-Ji Jeong explains the Korean alphabet as follows:

'This writing system can be mastered within hours by an wise person. It also can be learned within ten days by a foolish man.'

That means that the Korean alphabet is so simple that it can be mastered within a half day because it was created in a scientific way. A literacy rate of 100% in Korea is related to the fact that the Korean alphabet is easy to learn.

The Korean alphabet has proved its greater merits since the world entered the 21st century, called the digital era. Typing Korean on a computer is faster and more accurate compared to Chinese or Japanese. This is because in the Korean mode, all the consonants are entered by the left hand and all the vowels are entered by the right hand. It takes only 5 minutes to send off one Korean sentence using a mobile phone. So, in South Korea it is a habit with the young generation to exchange text messages on a mobile phone. The convenience of the Korean alphabet enabled South Korea to become a powerful country of the IT industry today.

Third, the Korean alphabet is a writing system which was not influenced by other writing systems but was ingeniously created. It is a phonemic script as well as a phonetic script. By constant studies on the vocal organs, its consonant characters were designed to depict the actual places of articulation of the phonological sounds these consonants represent. Its 3 basic vowel characters the dot '•', the horizontal '—' and the vertical ' | ' were patterned after Heaven, Earth and Man, respectively. There were 28 letters when the Korean alphabet was invented. But, after its creation, 4 letters were removed. Only 24 letters (10 vowels and 14 consonants) are used now.

Fourth, the Korean alphabet is easy to learn because it is a scientific writing system made by combining characters according to certain rules.

The 5 basic consonants 'ㄱ' (*gi yeok* 기역, presumably the weak /k/ as in "kid"), 'ㄴ' (*ni eun* 니은, presumably the /n/ as in "net"), 'ㅁ' (*mi eum* 미음, presumably the /m/ as in "man"), 'ㅅ' (*si ot* 시옷, presumably the /s/ as in "sky") and 'ㅇ' (*i eung* 이응, the /zero/ placed in front of the vowels and operating as a silent) were shaped after vocal organs. The 4 aspirated sounds 'ㅋ' (*ki euk* 키읔, presumably the strong /k/ as in "Korea"), 'ㅌ' (*ti eut* 티읕, presumably the strong /t/ as in "tower"), 'ㅍ' (*pi eup* 피읖, presumably the strong /p/ as in "power") and 'ㅊ' (*chi eut* 치읓, presumably the strong /ch/ as in "chain") were invented by adding a horizontal stroke to the 4 consonants 'ㄱ', 'ㄷ', 'ㅂ' and 'ㅈ' (*ji eut* 지읒, presumably the weak /ch/ sound as in "chin"), respectively. Further, the five tense consonants 'ㄲ' (*ssang gi yeok* 쌍기역, presumably the /k/ occurring after /s/ as in "sky"), 'ㄸ' (*ssang di geut* 쌍디귿, presumably the /t/ occurring after the /s/ as in "star"), 'ㅃ' (*ssang bi eup* 쌍비읍, presumably the /p/ occurring after the /s/ as in "spin"), 'ㅆ' (*ssang si ot* 쌍시옷, presumably the /s/ occurring before a vowel as in "sorry") and 'ㅉ' (*ssang ji eut* 쌍지읒, no similar sound in English) were invented by doubling the five consonants 'ㄱ', 'ㄷ', 'ㅂ', 'ㅅ' and 'ㅈ.' The vowels were invented by adding a vertical line to the 3 basic vowel phonemes or other vowels. That shows that the Korean alphabet can form an infinite number of syllables by combining 8 phonemes consisting basic consonants and vowels. So, the Korean alphabet is not only a phonemic script but also a syllabary which is a set of written symbols that represent syllables. For example, the word '*gang* 강 (river)' is a syllable form into which three phonemes the consonant 'ㄱ', the vowel 'ㅏ' and the consonant 'ㅇ' were combined.

Finally, the Korean alphabet has a remarkable ability with regard to phonetic representation.

According to the *hun min jeong eum* manuscript, the Korean alphabet can represent virtually all sounds that can be written down, including wind sound, the song of crane, a rooster's crowing sound and the sound of a dog. It can represent most fully the pronunciation of foreign languages. The Korean alphabet, consisting of only 24 letters (10 vowels and 14 consonants), can represent almost all of onomatopoeic and mimetic words. Here are a few examples of romanization for the Korean alphabet.

한글 → Hangeul
안녕하세요? → *An Nyeong Ha Se Yo?*
감사합니다. → *Gam Sa Hap Ni Da.*
사랑해요! → *Sa Rang He Yo!*

Korean Alphabet System

한글의 체계							
자음 (닿소리)	ㄱ 기역	ㄴ 니은	ㄷ 디귿	ㄹ 리을	ㅁ 미음	ㅂ 비읍	ㅅ 시옷
	ㅇ 이응	ㅈ 지읒	ㅊ 치읓	ㅋ 키읔	ㅌ 티읕	ㅍ 피읖	ㅎ 히읗
	ㅏ 아	ㅑ 야	ㅓ 어	ㅕ 여	ㅗ 오	ㅛ 요	ㅜ 우 ㅠ 유 ㅡ 으 ㅣ 이

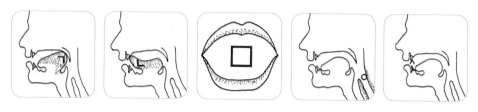

	글자를 만드는 원리	보기
자음	자음 기본 글자에 획을 더한다 기본 글자를 겹쳐 쓴다.	ㄱ→ㅋ ㄴ→ㄷ, ㅌ ㅁ→ㅂ, ㅍ ㅅ→ㅈ, ㅊ ㅇ→ㅎ ㄱ→ㄲ ㄴ→ ㄸ ㅁ→ ㅃ ㅅ→ㅆ, ㅉ
모음	모음 기본 글자를 합한다.	·+ㅡ=ㅗ, ㅜ(뒤집기) ·+ㅣ=ㅏ, ㅓ (뒤집기) ㅣ+ㅗ=ㅛ, ㅠ(뒤집기) ㅣ+ㅏ=ㅑ, ㅕ (뒤집기)
음절	자음과 모음을 합한다.	ㅁ+ㅏ+ㄹ=말 ㄲ+ㅗ+ㅊ=말

3. Characteristics of the Korean language and Korean people

First, in the Korean language there are various address terms and a developed honorific system.

Once upon a time relatives lived in the same village in the agricultural society of Korea. Because Korean people generally met their relatives in the village, terms of kinship relations instead of name were used as address terms. For example, the English word 'aunt' is translated into Korean words such as 'keun eo meo ni 큰어머니 (father's elder brother's wife)', 'jak eun eo meo ni 작은어머니 (father's younger brother's wife)', 'go mo 고모 (father's sister)', 'i mo 이모 (mother's sister)' and 'a ju meo ni 아주머니 (wife of the cousin of father)', according to closeness or remoteness of chon su 촌수 (kinship).

The Korean language has a highly developed honorific system, including honorific particles and suffixes. When the hearer is older than the speaker, the speaker must use honorific forms in place of regular ones. There are some words which refer to the same subject and whose use depends on the three politeness levels honorific, plain and humble. If the hearer is superior to the speaker in status, '*jin ji* 진지' is used instead of '*bap* 밥' for 'food.' And, the speaker uses (2) other than (1) for 'My father was angry.' when talking about his or her father.

(1) *apeoci-ka hwa-lul nae-ss-ta* (아버지가 화를 냈다).
father-NM anger-AC make-PST-DC
(2) *apeo-nim-kkeseo hwa-lul nae-syeo-ss-ta* (아버님께서 화를 내셨다).
father-HT-NM-HT anger-AC make-SH-PST-DC
(AC: accusative particle, DC: declarative sentence-type suffix, HT: honorific title, NM: nominative particle. and PST: past tense suffix)

Those examples show the diversity of terms of kinship relations and the development of honorific system in the Korean language. From this, it can derived from that Korean people put emphasis on their family and kin-groups. So, many Korean people regard language etiquette as a standard of refinement.

Second, there are abundant words expressing emotions or feelings in Korean.

Korean people are good at expressing their feelings and emotions minutely because the Korean language is a adjective- and adverb-developed language. They express the degree of pain in their back by using various emotive adjectives, such as '*ppeo geun ha da* 뻐근하다 (feel stiff)', '*kuk kuk ssu sin da* 쿡쿡 쑤신다 (tingle with pain)', '*tta kkeum geo rin da* 따끔거린다 (sting)', *jji ppu dung ha da* 찌뿌둥하다 (feel uncomfortable)' and '*kkeunh eo jil geot gat ta* 끊어질 것 같다 (I think the waist is broken).' The Korean language has a great variety of words expressing feelings. The color yellow is expressed not only in '*no rat da* 노랗다' but also in '*saet no ran eun haeng ip* 샛노란 은행잎 (deep-yellow ginkgo leaf)', '*no reu seu reum ha ge jal gu un ppang* 노르스름하게 잘 구운 빵 (bread baked to a golden brown)', '*nu reot ge tteun eol gul* 누렇게 뜬 얼굴 (sallow face)', '*no reut no reut ha ge gu eun gim* 노릇노릇하게 구운 김 (laver toasted to a golden brown)' and '*nu reon hwang so* 누런 황소 (golden yellow bull)', according to circumstances. Korean adverbs '*pong dang* 퐁당 (with a plop)' and '*pung deong* 풍덩 (with a plop)' show that they have different connotations. According to the vowel harmony rule in Korean, a bright vowel (e.g. 'ㅗ (/o/)') occurs only with a bright one (e.g. 'ㅏ') and a dark vowel (e.g. 'ㅜ') occurs only with a dark one (e.g. 'ㅓ') in those adverbs. So, Koean people are sensitive to feelings and emotions about words when they have a conversation, sing a song, or watch a movie. This sensitivity can be the motive of creating Korean good popular songs or movies which touch foreigners' heart.

Finally, there are various methods of word formation in Korean.

There are native Korean words and Sino-Korean words (derived from Chinese) in Korean vocabulary. For example, '*bul ssang* 불쌍' and '*ga ryeon* 가련 (可憐)' are a native Korean and a Sino-Korean word, respectively. Besides, many Korean words were created by blending two words a Sino-Korean word and a native Korean word, as follows:

(3) *gang* 강 江 (river) + *mul* 물 (water) → *gang mul* 강물 (water of rivers)
(4) *seon geo* 선거 選擧 (election) + *cheol* 철 (season) → *seon geo cheol* 선거철 (election season)

As shown above, Korean people have blended a lot of words to create a new word since early times. This shows that Korean people have a real feel for languages.

Nowadays, there are many combinations of a Sino-Chinese word and a loanword from English, as bellow:

(5) *jae* 재 財 (asset) + *te keu* 테크 (technology) → *jae te keu* 재테크 (asset management technology)

(6) *sing geul* 싱글 (single) + *jok* 족 族 (party) → *sing geul jok* 싱글족 (single people)

(7) *so gae* 소개 紹介 (introduction) + *ting* 팅 (meeting) → *so gae ting* 소개팅 (blind date)

Recently Korean young people enjoy blending Korean words thanks to the development of the internet, as follows:

(8) *eol gul* 얼굴 (face) + *jjang* 짱 (the best) → *eol jjang* 얼짱 (beautiful person)

(9) *yeol sim hi* 열심히 (diligently) + *gong bu ha da* 공부하다 (study) → *yeol gong* 열공 (studying hard)

South Korea is one of the countries which have many archival heritages in the world. This is closely related to a national characteristic of Korean people who enjoy privileges of human language and scripts. Korean people had noble consciousness and a culture of classical scholar because they placed high value on study from old times. Today, the zeal for children's education in South Korea is considerably high.

Exercises

01 Read the following explanations. If they are right, put O in the
brackets next to them. If they are wrong, put X instead.
1) Korea is a peninsula state which has a long history of 5,000 years. (　)
2) The national flag of South Korea is the Korean flag with the central
tae geuk pattern. Its national flower is rose. (　)
3) South Korea is now a divided country and its capital is Seoul. (　)
4) It is rude not to use proper polite expressions depending on the
hearer or the subject when you have a talk with someone in Korean.
5) Korea has its own language and script different from ones of its two
neighboring countries China and Japan. (　)

02 Write Korea's public holidays to the best of your ability.

03 Write five reasons why the hun min jeong eum manuscript on the
writing system was registered as the UNESCO World
Documentary Heritage in 1997 on the ground that the Korean
alphabet is the most superior writing system in the world.

04 There were two events praised by foreign presses after 1990 in the modern history of Korea. Briefly explain them.

05 Write expressions for Korea's past and present 'images.' Talk to others about reasons why those images were created.

There are many beauties in Korea because it has clean water!

Step 1 Geography and Climate

1. Geography

Mountains and rivers

There are many mountains in the Korean Peninsula.

Low hills and mountains account for about 70% of Korean territory. They can be found anywhere. Water flows in a valley, and rice fields and farms fill the countryside. This natural scenery offers a friendly atmosphere because it reminds people of a mother's breast. Mountains are very familiar to Korean people. There are so many people in South Korea who like mountains that on holidays cities near mountains are crowded with mountain hikers from morning.

The topography of the Korean Peninsula resembles the powerful back of a tiger. The largest mountain in Korea is Paekdu Mountain (2744m). *Paek du dae gan* 백두대간 is the backbone of the Korean Peninsula which runs through the range of the Taebaek Mountains, stretching along the coast of the East Sea from Paekdu Mountain in the north to Jiri Mountain in the south. *Paek du dae gan* has a high-east and low-west topography that the northern and eastern part of it is mainly mountainous but the southern and western part of it has many plains and rivers.

In the Korean Peninsula there are many rivers running along ranges of

Mountains and plains of Korea
Topography of Korean Peninsula resembling tiger

mountains. The Han River is a representative one. The Han River originates in a small mountain stream of Gwangweon Province and flows through Seoul and Incheon into the Yellow Sea joining many branch rivers as it flows downstream. Rice farming techniques developed around the Han River as plains were formed by high-quality river sediment and alluvial soil. There were also porcelain production sites, such as Yeoju and Icheon. The Han River is used as a source of drinking water for people in Seoul and its surrounding areas because the river has plenty of water.

The Nakdong River is the longest river in the southern part of Korea and the lifeline of the Gyeongsang Province. It flows through Daegu, a textile industrial city, and Busan into the South Sea.

The Yeongsan River flows through the Jeolla Provinces. The Honam

(Jeolla Province) Plain was formed at the basin of the Yeongsan River. There are so rice paddies in the plain that it is called 'rice granary of Korea.'

Seas and islands

The Korean Peninsula is surrounded by water on the three sides the East Sea, the South Sea and the West Sea (the Yellow Sea). Compared to the East Sea, the coastlines of the South Sea and the West Sea have more complex because they have a lot of islands large and small.

There are a lot of tourist attractions in the East Sea whose open sea connected to the Pacific is harmonized with the scenery of the Taebaek Mountains. Beaches in the East Sea are very crowded in summer. Because there is a lot of snow on mountains facing the sea, ski resorts on them open in winter.

Because warm and cold currents meet in the East Sea, various types of fish species are abundant in this area. The representative ones of them are pollack and squid. Korean people enjoy eating both of them as a side dish or a light meal. Dried pollack is called *boog eo* 북어. Korean people enjoy eating a fish soup called *boog eo guk* 북어국 as a hangover soup to get over a hangover. Squid is a very nutritious food, containing protein and calcium. Especially, well dried squids are enjoyed as a snack because they are salty and chewy. Dried squids spark Korean people's memories of childhood. They listened to their grandmother's great old time stories chewing a dried squid when cookies were not common. A dried squid is enjoyed as a side dish in a lunch box or an accompaniment to drink.

There are *Ulleungdo* 울릉도 (Ulleung Island), the second largest island in Korea, and *Dokdo* 독도 (Dok Island), an island, in the East Sea. Dok Island is the easternmost location of the administrative district in Korea. As an administrative district, the actual address is 63 Isabu-gil, Dokdo-li, Ulleung-eup, Ulleung-gun, Gyeongsangbuk-do, South Korea. The place name 'Isabu-gil' is derived from the historical fact that Dok Island was

Squid drying in Danghae

subjugated to Korea by General Isabu during the reign of King Jijeung (437-514), a ruller of the Shilla Kingdom, in the Three Kingdoms Period. In recent years, the whole country have a great concern of serving as a Dokdo keeper which was started to care Dok island and to maintain what our forefathers left us. Dok Island had about 2,000 habitants in as of 2007; so, it is not a lonely island any more.

There are many great and small islands in the South Sea. Jeju Island, the largest island in Korea, is situated on the South Sea. Jeju Island is famous tourist site because it is a volcanic island and its scenery is beautiful beyond all descriptions. Jeju Island is also famous for a major producer of tangerines. The South Sea is not deep and its temperature is suitable for aquaculture industries. Oyster farming and laver farming have made great developments in Jeju Island. Jeju-made seaweed laver is of good quality. A lot of dried laver products made in Jeju are exported to its neighbor country Japan. Korean people enjoy eating as a side dish dried laver seasoned with sesame oil and salt and roasted. They make *gim bap* 김밥 (seasoned rice rolled in a sheet of seaweed) as a substitute of lunch on their travels. Gim bap is a delicious and nutritious meal because it was concocted from dried laver, steamed rice and different kinds of vegetables.

The West Sea has a large tidal range. The West Sea is called 'the Yellow Sea.' The name 'the Yellow Sea' is derived from its color. It has been said that the Yellow River in China causes the West Sea to yellow. Incheon and Mokpo, port cities along the West Sea, were places where trade between

Korean and China was active in old times. Today many ships use sea routes from the two port cities to Shangdong Province and other areas in China. Croaker is one of the West Sea's specialties. Especially, croaker fished near Yeonpyeong Island was served for kings in the old days because it tastes delicious and is of superior quality.

2. Climate

Korea has four distinct seasons: spring, summer, autumn and winter.

Korea has a continental climate characterized by annual variation in temperature. The annual mean temperature in Korea is 10-16℃. The average temperature in August, the hottest period of the year, ranges from 23℃ to 27℃, while in January, the coldest month, temperatures range from −6℃ to −7℃. Korea's annual average precipitation is 1200-1300mm and higher than the global average.

In Korea, spring (March to May) is warm. In May there are so many different kinds of beautiful flowers galore in the whole of Korea that May is called 'the Queen of Seasons.' There is a cold snap during the flowering season. Yellow sand dust blows down from mainland China every spring.

Summer (June to August) in Korea is sultry. In the rainy season, the high relative humidity causes hot and humid weather. Daegu is the hottest place in Korea and the highest temperature in summer was 40 degrees above zero.

Autumn (September to November) is cool. Mountains and fields covered with varicolored autumn leaves attract tourists. In autumn, the sky is high and blue and the air is very fresh. The average temperature in October is 11-19℃. Autumn is the season of great harvests of fresh fruits. The temperature and relative humidity are good for outdoor activities or the ripening of grains and fruits. Fruits taste sweet and delicious. Korean people eat fruits raw.

Winter (December to February) is cold. During the winter time, the temperature remains below zero because of bone-chilling winds from Siberia lying northwest of Korea. But, some days actually feel like spring. There is a saying for this and it is called 'sam han sa on 삼한사온' that means a cycle of three cold days and four warm days. Junggangjin is the coldest place in the Korean Peninsula and the lowest temperature in winter was 20 degrees below zero. It snows in winter and it is so beautiful. Because of a lot of snow in winter, Gangweon-do has popular snow-covered ski resorts and winter sights.

Korean people are generally energetic and diligent because they live in a continental climate characterized by hot summers and cold winters. The seasons' weather is clearly different. Korea has so beautiful, different scenery in each season that people can enjoy travelling all year round. The beauties of nature stimulate Korean people's emotion and are the main factor in their formation of various living cultures.

• Plum blossom in spring •• Valleys in summer ••• Rice harvesting in autumn •••• Mountain in winter

Step 2 Nature and Korean People

1. Land, water and Korean people

The mountains of Korea are covered with thick forests.

Trees take water from the ground through their roots although heavy rain falls. Little by little trees emit water which forms a stream. The water quality in Korea is very good because evenly bedded strata filter rain water well. In the old days, the water from rivers or streams were fit to drink. Wherever people dug, it became a clear pool of drinkable spring water. Korean people's habits were created by their geographical environment such as beautiful mountains and clean water, as shown below.

First, Korean people enjoyed drinking water without boiling it. Today they heat the tap water before drinking it. They still like drinking mineral water.

Second, Korean people enjoy watery foods. Korean foods are characterized by soup or stock. Because almost all of these foods are wet, Korean bowls are very concave in shape. Korean people have the habit of having breakfast with soup.

Third, Korean people enjoy eating fresh vegetables and fruits raw. This means that there is a lot of water to wash fruits in several changes of it. Korean people hardly eat fried or boiled fruits. They like eating boiled rice wrapped in clean vegetables. Broiled meat or three-layered port wrapped in leaves of lettuce is considered to be a delicacy.

Fourth, Korea has been known as a beauty-obsessed country. In Korea there are old sayings such as '*nam nam buk nyeo* 남남북녀' and '*pyeong yang gi saeng* 평양기생.' The one means that handsome men are found in the south and the beautiful women in the north. The other means that *gi saeng* 기생 (professional singing and dancing women in Korean traditional society) born in Pyeongang, a city on the north side of the Korean Peninsula, is the most beautiful in Korea. These old sayings tell us that there are many beautiful women in the north. Geographically, the north area of the Korean Peninsula is more mountainous than the south. Clean water runs off the surface, down the Nangrim Mountains eventually into the Taedong River, which flows through Pyeongyang, the quality of water in Pyeongyang is good. Because clean water is good for skin, there are so many beautiful women in Pyeongyang. Foreigners who visited Korea say that Korea has many beautiful women. Some of them wrongly believe that the reason is that Korean women are good at makeup or those women are artificial plastic beauties. However, most of Korean beautiful women are natural beauties. As the saying, 'you can't polish a turd', a good skin is essential for makeup.

Fifth, Korean people tend to use a lot of water. There is the expression 'spend money like water' in Korean. As it shows, Korean people use plenty of water. Korean foods have various types of soups or stocks. For example, a lot of meat stock is added to *naeng myeon* 냉면 (Korean cold noodles). Korean people cannot drink up the stock and any left is thrown out. Many Korean people enjoy going to spas or saunas causing large water consumption to relax their body and soul. Bathing culture for skin care and relaxation is one of the most popular tourist attractions in South Korea.

Finally, Korean people are those who praise the nature and who are simple and honest. Korean soil is called 'ok to 옥토', which means rich soil. Because the soil is moist and fertile, Korean people can have a good harvest. People did not need to worry about drinking, for every place they dug became a clear pool of drinkable spring water. So, they do not covet what belongs to others. Rather, they think that it is included in a happy life to praise the nature, are content amid poverty and take delight in the Taoist Way. This can be found in old poems or songs. Also, the national characteristic of loving peace can be drawn from the historical fact that Korean people did not invade other countries to meet their needs.

2. Weather and Korean people

Korea belongs to the temperate zone suitable to live in.

Korean people care about their dress and are sensitive to different weathers and sceneries of each season because Korean has four distinct seasons. These weathers influence Korean people's characteristics, as follows.

First, Korean people have an exceptional sense of style.

The temperature change throughout the year has a great effect on clothing life. Korean people made thin and cool clothes for summer and cotton-filled warm clothes for winter. Because Korean people make clothes of different styles for every type of weather, they change soiled clothes into clean ones. This shows that Korean people are diligent. Generally, Korean people believe that first impression depends on the cut of jib in relationships. They try to be properly dressed according to occasion and location. They believe that the cut of jib is an important etiquette to maintain a good relationship with other people because there is the old saying, 'Neat and tidy dress comes from a neat mental attitude towards others.'

Korean people have a lot of interest in colors of clothes and an exceptional sense of style because they grow up in the environment of different colors of the nature of each season. Today, clothes made by Korean people are popular in world markets. This is related to the natural environment of Korea which has four distinct seasons.

Second, Korean people have a highly-developed aesthetic sense in the fields of music and movie because they are sensitive to their feelings.

It has been said that people who live in a lovely weather have a relatively developed sense of arts. There are plenty of sunny days in Italy, located in the shores of the Mediterranean. Italy is internationally known as a country of music because Italian people like expressing these sunny days through songs.

In spring and autumn, temperatures in South Korea are comfortable. The sky is so blue and clean that Korean people find themselves humming. Especially, the autumn sky in Korea is famous for the cleanest and bluest one in the world. People's mood vary according to the weather. Appreciating weather, Korean people frequently sing a song or poem softly to themselves. When it snows for the first time, the volume of telephone calls becomes so massive that telecommunication networks are paralyzed. On the day, radio or TV stations broadcast music or memories on the first snow of the season, expressing the spirit and mind to assimilate into the nature.

Korean TV dramas, songs and dances have become so popular worldwide that the words 'the Korean Wave' and 'K-pop' came in. This reflects Korean people's artistic sensitivity cultivated by lovely weather. Korean movies are set in mountains, the sea and islands of Korea in all seasons of the year. The landscape of those places moves cinema audiences because it is as pretty as a picture. Film locations are actually popular tourist attractions visited by a great number of people. Those people show their mental state of acting like the main character in the location of a movie.

Third, Korean people are diligent.

Korea has four distinct seasons and each season passes relatively quickly. Following the change of seasons, Korean farmers have done farm diligently because the crops fail if one of the farming steps is missed. For example, although Korean farmers drink alcohol and sing a song in a rainy day, all of them sow seeds in a field if 'the sowing season' begin on the following day according to the lunar calendar. In Korea the farming steps are done based on the 24 seasonal divisions, the 24 divisions of the year. So, Korean farmers develop diligence naturally, while doing farm according to the divisions.

Step 3 Administration District and Population

1. Metropolitan cities and provincial divisions

South Korea is divided seven metropolitan cities and nine provinces. First of all, the seven metropolitan cities are Seoul, Busan, Daegu, Incheon, Daejeon, Gwangju and Ulsan. Then, the nine provinces are Gyeonggi-do, Gangweon-do, Chungcheong-bukdo, Chungcheong-namdo, Gyeongsang-bukdo, Gyeongsang-namdo, Jeolla-bukdo, Jeolla-namdo and Jeju-do.

Seoul, Incheon and Gyeonggi-do

The city through which the

Administrative guidance

Night view of N Seoul Tower of the Mt. Nam

lifeline of the Korean economy flows slowly and which achieved 'Miracle on the Han River!'

This is the capital city Seoul, the heart of South Korea. Seoul is the major political, economical and cultural center of South Korea. Seoul is an international city where the Olympics took place in 1988 and the FIFA World Cup was held in 2002. Seoul looks like a modernized city now, but it is an old city which has kept 600 years of history since it became the capital of Joseon in 1394. Traditional culture and modern culture coexist in Seoul because there are traditional palaces and historical sites here and there in the city's forest of buildings.

In terms of geomantic principles, Seoul is placed at an auspicious location where it is surrounded by Mt. Bukhan and the Han River flows through it.

Han River giving relaxation in the urban life

Foreigners visiting Seoul say that the Han River is very impressive because there are scarcely large rivers, such as the Han River, which flow through a capital city in the world. The Han River is a beautiful gift of nature which sweetens our breath and let us forget our loneliness.

Through Incheon, the gateway city of the Yellow Sea, Korea has made vigorous exchanges with China and other countries since old times. As the leading industrial city around Seoul, Incheon is good location for manufacture and distribution. For the first time in Korea, a railway line was built in 1899 and it connected Seoul to Incheon. The Incheon International Airport, which was opened in 2001, shows that Incheon has an aspect of international city.

Busan, Daegu, Gyeongsang-namdo and Gyeongsang-bukdo

Gyeongsang-do, 'the home of apples and beauties', is the place through which the history of the Silla period. Gyeongsang-do is called the Yeongnam region. Daegu is the central city of Gyeongsang-bukdo, and it is well known for apple production and textile industry. The Nakdong River flows around Daegu. It is said that Daegu has a lot of beauties because the water in the Nakdong River is clean and they enjoy eating apples. Busan is the second largest city in South Korea after Seoul. Busan is famous for popular attractions such as Haeundae Beach Resort. The fishing industry has made great developments in Busan. The Busan International Film Festival is held every year in a beautiful natural environment alongside the beach.

Gwangju, Jeolla-namdo and Jeolla-bukdo

Jeolla-do, 'the home of taste and songs', is southwest of the Korean Peninsula. Jeolla-do is called the Honam region. This region has produces a lot of rice since old times because most of it occupy open fields. Jeolla-do, which meets the sea, are rich in marine products in addition to agricultural products. The food culture in Jeolla-do has so greatly developed that most famous restaurant owners are regarded as being from it. Also, musical arts such as folk songs and *pan so ri* 판소리 (traditional Korean narrative song) are developed in Jeolla-do. This region has been called 'the home of arts' since old times. The Gwanju Kimchi Cultural Festival is annually held in Gwangju, a representative city of the Honam region,

Gangweon-do

Gangweon-do, 'the tourist attraction with mountains and beaches', has a lot of beautiful mountains such as Mt. Seorak and Mt. Taebaek. Gangweon-do is famous as a summer resort for the people of Seoul because mountains meet the East Sea in this region. In winter there is a lot of snow in the region. Many people enjoy winter sports such as ski there.

Daejeon, Chungcheong-namdo and Chungcheong-bukdo

Chungcheong-do, the region containing 'the capital of the Baekje Kingdom', has a lot of historical remains such as *nak hwa am* 낙화암, which literally means 'a rock over the river.' In Chungcheong-do there is also the Independence Memorial Hall. Chungcheong-do is the region where the three regions meet: the Seoul metropolitan region, the Yeongnam region and the Honam region. Chungcheong-do has been the transport center of Korea since old times. Daejeon, a representative city of Chungcheong-do, is a major transportation point of South Korea.

Jeju-do

Jeju-do, 'the exotic vacation spot', is the largest island in South Korea. Jeju Island is a volcanic island. Mountains and caves made from the lava flow traces have a unique appearance. Because Jeju Island has a maritime climate, it is warm here all the year round. In spring the rape flowers are so in full blossom on Jeju Island that the surrounding area of the island turns yellow. Mt. Halla is located in the center of Jeju Island and the top of it is covered with snow even in spring. The contrastive scenes of yellow and white colors are also the beauty of Jeju Island. This island is famous as a honeymoon resort because of its exotic scenery. Jeju-do is a tourist resort designated as an international tourist zone.

2. Administrative units and public institutions

South Korea has three administrative tiers. The first tier includes seven metropolitan cities and nine provinces. In the second administrative tier, provinces are subdivided into small cities, *gu* 구 (borough) and *gun* 군 (county). The third administrative tier consists of subdivisions of cities or

Korean registration card

ID card of South Korea

Certificate of alien registration (front side)

Certificate of alien registration (back side)

dong 동 (ward), and subdivisions of rural counties into *eup* 읍 (town), *myeon* 면 (township) and *ri* 리. A ward office (or community center) is in charge of the most basic administrative duties in the city. The ward office actually offers administrative services such as issue of registration card, moving-in and out notification, and military service notification. Now, with the development of the internet, official documents can be issued by any ward offices in South Korea.

Korean people must be issued a registration card (identification card) when they become 17 years old. The system of registration of family relationship was established after the patriarchal family system was abolished in 2008. A certificate of family relations or a marriage certificate is issued by the ward office. The registration card is expected to be replaced by the identification card of the Republic of Korea.

In South Korea there are public institutions, such as police station, fire station and post office in addition to ward office. As multicultural families increase in South Korea, various foreigner policies are being carried out. Korea Immigration Service (http://www.immigration.go.kr) has control over those policies. A foreigner who wants to stay in South Korea for 90 days or longer must obtain a certificate of alien registration. The certificate is issued by the immigration office which has jurisdiction over the locality where the foreigner is residing. Immigration Contact Center (ph: 1345) offers a lot of services to foreigners staying in South Korea. The center supplies counselling services in 18 foreign languages.

The telephone number of emergency call center is 119. Packages are sent to another place or country via the post office. A parcel delivery company collects packages from the customer's home or office if he or she orders by telephone.

3. Population

The total population of South and North Korea exceeds seventy million. South Korea has the 20th largest population in the world with fifty million four thousand people. The population density is ranked as the 3rd in the world, following Bangladesh and Taiwan.

In particular, Seoul is so crowded with people. Sometimes people bump against each other on the street. When it happens, they leave a word of excuse and go their way rather than stop and apologize. This phenomenon comes from it high population density.

By 1950, the age structure of South Korea was an expensive population pyramid that is very wide at the base, indicating high birth and death rates. As a result of the rapid economic development in South Korea and its family planning program after that time, the expensive pyramid changed to a constrictive pyramid that is a typical pattern for a very developed country which has a low death rate as well as a low birth rate and whose population is generally older on average. Generally, the traditional extended family system in South Korea is breaking up in favor of the nuclear family consisting of a pair of adults and their one or two children.

The ratio between men and women in South Korea is 101.6 to 100.0 and men preponderate a little in number. It is expected that in the future South Korea will have a preponderance of women members because of the social phenomenon of weak preference for male offsprings and of the average life expectancy of men shorter than that of women.

The average life expectancy of Korean people was 79.1 in 2006. The average life span of men and women is 77.3 and 84, respectively. This shows that women live 7 years longer than men.

The age of marriage in South Korea is gradually rising. According to Korea National Statistical Office (KNSO), the average age at marriage for men and women is respectively 27.8 and 24.8 in the 1990s. KNSO released the report that the average age at marriage for men and women is respectively 30.9 and 27.8 in 2006. Compared to the 1990s, the average age of marriage in 2006 is about 3 years higher. This is related to the working age of young people. The average of working age for Korean people is 27. Especially, the working age of men is higher than that of women because men serve in the military and graduate from a university. The age of marriage for women is gradually rising as they are shifting their consciousness into taking employment after university graduation for granted.

Exercises

01 Read the following explanations. If they are right, put O in the brackets next to them. If they are wrong, put X instead.

1) Because Korea contains many mountains, they can be found anywhere. (　)

2) The Han River flows through the middle of Seoul and Incheon into the Yellow Sea. (　)

3) In Korea, it rains a little in summer but a lot in winer. (　)

4) Because South Korea does not have a high density of population, only a few people live in the country. (　)

5) There are Ulleung Island 울릉도 (Ulleungdo), the second largest island in Korea, and Dok Island 독도 (Dokdo), an island, in the East Sea. (　)

02 Choose the area that best describes the following explanation and insert the symbol between the brackets.

> Examples a. Seoul b. Jeju-do c. Jeolla-do d. Incheon e. Daegu f. Busan

1) The heart of South Korea and the city where the Olympics took place in 1988 and which achieved 'Miracle on the Han River' (   )
2) The gateway city of the Yellow Sea, the international airport city and the leading industrial city (   )
3) The breadbasket of South Korea and the region famous for its delicious foods (   )
4) A volcanic island, an exotic vacation spot with Mt. Halla as its center (   )

03 What is the thing that Korean people must be issued when they become 17 years old? And, what is the identification card that a foreigner who wants to stay in South Korea for 90 days or longer must obtain?

04 Write influences of weather on Korean people to the best of your ability.

05 Korea has been called 'A country with beautiful mountains and clean water' since old times. Find relevant examples from Korean people's eating habits and lifestyle and explain why.

Chapter

3

Family and Manners

Why do Korean people always ask people's age when they meet for the first time?

Step 1 Characteristics of Korean Families

1. Filial piety

There is the fairy tale 'Chung Shim, the Filial Daughter' in Korea.

The story is about a young daughter who sacrificed her life for her blind father. It tells us that Korean people consider their family (parents and children), as 'a group bound together by a common destiny for which their life can be devoted.'

According to a press' survey in 2005, Korean people's idea on family as seen by foreigners is as follows:

'Korean people take pride in their familism enough to become a model to other countries. Their devotion and duties to their family are becoming a guideline in all areas of Korean society, regardless of age, sex, social class and rank. It was seen as the medium that unites Korean people by a strong community ethics.'

Characteristics of Korean traditional families were greatly influenced by Confucianism of the Joseon period. As it is said that all goes well when one's home is harmonious, that is, the peace in a family is a prerequisite for the prosperity of a country, the family and family life was highly regarded

Close family

by Confucian ethics. To the present day, characteristics of family have been passed down which put emphasis on the patriarch- and superior-oriented norms and filial duty. For example, there are seats in the subways of South Korea that are designated as seats for seniors. Also, senior citizens do not pay for transportation.

Since old times, Korean people have observed strictly filial piety, duty of care for their parents, evaluating it as a very important human virtue. They thought what separates man from beast is the act to express thanks to his parents for bringing him into this world and respect his parents. They considered it as their duty. They thought with all his heart, a human ought to look into their parents day and night and hold a funeral, and a memorial service, for his deceased parents so as to be blessed. Some people built a mud hut next to their deceased parents' graveyard and then protected it from being desecrated for 3 years. Filial duty was established as society and nation as well as family. Farmers considered it as an observance of filial piety, to do farming diligently, live with and support their parents, and pay the tax properly.

From a perspective of the relationship between duties and rights established by parents and their children in Korea, filial piety is interpreted as the structure where parents look after their children and then they are taken care of by their children when they become old. That is to say, parents in South Korea do not mind giving financial support to their children before their children graduate from a university and get married. Generally, parents in South Korea are supported by their children for the rest of their life not until their children earn enough money to help them in a society. On the other hand, people in the West are financially independent of their family and pay for their tuition with the money they earn when they enter college. In general, people in the West are rarely responsible for supporting their aged parents. Instead, the government solves problems of aging on the level of social welfare. It is said that people of other countries envy of Korean people for characteristics of their family because most countries solve those problems by the latter method. In South Korea, three generations of the family live together through thick and thin and love one another. This can be called an 'ideal life.'

2. Elder-centered community and rank-oriented consciousness

'Why do Korean people always ask people's age when they meet for the first time?'

Foreigners often ask me this question because they consider it to be rude to ask that to a person they meet for the first time. Korean people rarely call someone by his name. Instead they ask him his age or title to call him by a proper term of address. This is language manner and language custom of Korea.

This language custom is influenced by a large family system and Confucianism of the Joseon period. In the past all members of village belonged to a single kinship group. The leader of large family group was the oldest person (or elder) in the village. The leader led the group while imparting wisdom on how to do farming and taking responsibilities in various family affairs such as marriage and funeral. A man should learn wisdom and virtue from the oldest man in his family so as to be an upright person in a society according to Confucian teaching.

The characteristic of elder-centered family is the emphasis on virtue of respecting elders, that is, rank-oriented consciousness where the young must honor their elders and precedence should be given to older people. It is a language manner for Korean people not to refer to family members by name. Younger siblings are not supposed to address their elders by name but by appellations, such as *sa chon hyeong* 사촌형 (older male cousin), *a jeo ssi* 아저씨 (father's cousin) and *oe suk mo* 외숙모 (wife of mother's brother), according to the degrees of kinship. This custom is applied to social life. When Korean people meet someone for the first time, they ask his or her age to call in a polite manner. That is to say, they are supposed to use proper words, greetings and attitudes for a situation when they are younger than the person. Korean people first ask people's age when they exchange names. It is rude to call the elder by his or her name. So, Korean people call the elder by appellations, such as *hyeong nim* 형님 (older brother), *seon saeng nim* 선생님 (sir), *sa jang nim* 사장님 (president) and *a jum ma* 아줌마 (ma'am).

The Korean language has a developed system of honorific endings, in addition to that of appellations. Korean people should use the honorific to observe their language manners. For example, lower grade students must use the honorific towards an upper grade student although they are one grade below him or her. Also, soldiers must use the honorific even towards a person who got assigned to the same unit several months earlier than them. The use of honorifics is an unwritten rule in Korea. This reminds me of the old saying, 'there is an order in drinking cool water.'

The youngers are supposed to show a politeness towards the elders according to Korean manners of honoring elders. When Korean people greet, the younger bows to the elder. When they drink alcohol, the younger drinks turning his or her head right. Also, the youngers do not smoke in front of the elders. Korean people sit and sleep on the floor. When the elder comes into a room, the younger stands up to bow the elder. Korean people are united by loyalty and obedience to family and society which come from rank-oriented consciousness and manners in the elder-centered community. On the other hand, saving face and authoritarian thought caused by both of them become an obstacle to equal conversation or free discussion.

3. Patriarchal society and sexual discrimination consciousness

'If a man is the sky, the woman is the earth.'

Korean people had patriarchal values only 50 years ago. It is not to much to say that Korean people's subconscious has had an emphasis on the eldest son based on men-oriented values which was established in the Joseon period. Patriarchal values that lie in contemporary Korean families are shown by the father of Daebal, the eldest son of the family in the Korean drama 'sa rang i mweo gil lae 사랑이 뭐길래 (What Is Love All About)', which was broadcasted in the prime time hour of China Central Television (CCTV) in 1998 and became an originator of Korean dramas that contributed to the Korean Wave.

Korean traditional families are patriarchal. Korean people take their father's last name. Men have the right of preference to make a claim to the head of a family or inheritance of property. More emphasis was put on the paternal line than the maternal line, including relatives on the mother's side of a family and the wife's family.

In Korea's patriarchal society, women were low in social status and did not take an important role in the family. Korean women are only supposed to be a wise mother and good wife. In particular, they have a large duty to give birth to a son to carry on the family line because of a marked preference for boys and a custom to have many children. They were taught a manner of obedience, as shown in the old saying, 'It goes ill with the house where the hen sings and the cock is silent.' They should not make a loud noise at home. It is rude that they visit other's house early. It was good form that men look down on their wife in front of others because they were considered as being masculine. They were impliedly taught that helping a woman work is not a behavior like a man while they were being prevented from going to the vicinity of the kitchen because it had been said that his penis is cut if a man goes into the kitchen.

However, these traditional values began to be varied after the pattern of family formation was changed from a large family to a small one by rapid industrialization and urbanization after the 1960s. The fertility in South Korea greatly dropped because of its population policy in the 1970s, well known as the family planning slogan 'Don't discriminate between boys and girls, have only two children and raise them well.' Accordingly, an increase in women's economic activities changed their attitudes towards work and marriage. Further, Men's attitudes towards women have changed from asserting their authority as a patriarch to cooperating with women since women had equal opportunities to men in education and women's economic activities became more common.

Recently, the change in traditional family pattern in South Korea led to the revision of the family law. It also led to the abolishment of the patriarchal family system and inheritance of property where the eldest is given priority. From outward appearances, it seems that Korean family patterns have changed greatly. But, Korean people's subconscious still bears patriarchal values.

4. Family community and 'we' consciousness

Let's visualize images of a Korean farm village.

Villages containing a cluster of houses were usually found in Korea. There was a small village which less than fifty households were clustered about in. There was another small village located near the village. Most of these villages was a form of community created by a large family consisting of 'a group of people who had a common ancestor.' When they moved out of their parents' house after their marriage, they lived just two doors away from their parents or eldest brother to create a village. That is to say, the village was a family community whose members had the same surname and were related

Korea's farm village

by blood. Most of Korean farm villages still consists of households that have the same surname these days. For example, there are two adjacent villages consisting of kinship groups. The one is a village located upwards where most members have the last name Park. The other is a village located downwards where most residents have the surname Papyeong Yoon.

In an agricultural society, a spirit of mutual cooperation was developed early because all members of a village were descended from a common ancestor. It increased labor productivity and rice production. At busy farming season, Korean people helped one another to grow rice while they turned setting out young rice plants and harvesting rice, depending on which day it was. When performing ancestral rites and others, they frequently met to strengthen their kinship. So, they could lead a life preserved and protected by the community rather than a personal life.

Agricultural society and kinship community structure are very important in understanding Korean people because both of them existed as Korea's life style for thousands of years. Today Korea is not an agricultural society, but in their subconscious mind, Korean people have a strong spirit of mutual help between members of the same kinship community. When one member of the community gets married or goes through mourning, other members give him or her money as a contribution for that. Also, if the member's son is accepted into a good university, other members raise the money to help him enter the university.

The concept of the community spirit was also applied to a society or a nation. It is 'we' consciousness. In particular, this consciousness was strengthened by the customs of Confucianism in the Joseon period. This can be seen from the fact that a family was honored above a person. In the Joseon period, when a person passed the civil service examination, it was considered an honor to his family. On the contrary, if the person was branded as a rebel or arrested for treason against the king, the three sets of relatives were exterminated on joint responsibility for it: relatives on his father's side, his mother's side and his wife's side. The movie 'Family's Honor' was played three years ago. Because the movie became a hit, it was followed by the movie 'Marrying the Mafia', whose original title is 'Family's Crisis.' This shows that Korean people have lived for the kinship community sharing a common destiny whose members live and die for their family called 'we.' Korean society was so greatly affected by 'we' consciousness that South Korea achieved an economic revival called the 'Miracle of the Han River' 30 years after the Korean War. That is to say, the miracle resulted from Korean people's contributing to their companies as they worked for their family. A company pays its employees for their work. But, Korean companies like persuading their employees to contribute to their success with a sense of familial warmth and kinship. When they educate their employees, they say, 'Let's share joys and sorrows together because we have lived under the same roof like a family.' They believe that employees with strong ties to their company are closely united and increase productivity.

Today 'we' consciousness was proved by two events: gold collection campaign and Korean people wearing red T-shirts to cheer their soccer team during the 2012 FIFA World Cup in Korea and Japan. First of all, the campaign enabled Korean people to get through the financial crisis in a short of period of time after Korea received $57 billion in bailout money from IMF in 1997. Then, Korean people with red T-shirts showed their persistence and passion again by cheering for their soccer team during the World Cup games. In those days, foreign media called the persistence and passion the flame of Korean people's patriotism. Korean people have a deeper emotion that cannot be expressed by the word 'patriotism.' It is 'we' consciousness that brings them together because it makes them think that the nation's business is their own. When the Korean team made it to the semi-finals at the 2012 FIFA World Cup in Korea and Japan, they were jubilant. Some of them offered goods, beverages or meals. This clearly shows 'we' consciousness inherent in Korean people.

The negative aspect of 'we' consciousness is exclusiveness. There is awkwardness when Korean people approach a stranger first. They did not have any vigorous interchanges with other countries. On the other hand, Korean people share a national characteristic of being warm-hearted. They are generous because they have taken over the tradition that the host should entertain guests in his place with all his hearts. Recently, there has been a rapid increase in the number of foreigners coming to marry Korean people, and study and work as well as multi-cultural families in South Korea. So, Korean people should show the spirit of an open community accepting different cultures and communities. It is time that under the idea that as a global village member people all around the world belong to one family, they need to exhibit the wisdom of living together in perfect harmony while inhering their own culture.

Web sites relating to 'multi-cultural families'

1. Korean Immigration Service http://www.immigration.go.kr
2. Multi-cultural Open Society http://www.multicos.co.kr
3. Seoul Global Center http://global.seoul.go.kr
4. Health Family Support Centers http://mfsc.familynet.or.kr
5. Support Center for Women's Hotline http://www.wm1366.or.kr
6. Salad TV Multicultural Broadcasting http://saladtv.kr
7. Korea Support Center for Foreign Workers http://www.migrantok.org
8. Center for Multicultural Education http://www.cme.or.kr
9. International Marriage and Family Support Center http://ifamilynet.or.kr
10. Center for Multi-cultural Korea http://www.cmck.kr
11. The Cyber University of Korea's Multicultural Campaign http://ecamp.kdu.edu
12. Network for Immigrants and Practitioners of Migration Management http://migrant.kr
13. Ministry of Gender Equality & Family http://www.mogef.go.kr
14. Ministry of Health & Welfare http://www.mw.go.kr
15. Women Migrant Humanrights Center http://www.wmigrant.org
16. Migrant Health Association in Korea http://mumk.org
17. Korea Multicultural Family Solidarity http://www.comfa.org
18. Rainbow Youth Center http://www.rainbowyouth.or.kr
19. Migrant Women & Multi-cultured Families Center http://eulim.org
20. Migrants' Network TV http://www.mntv.net

Step 2 Family Relations and Manners

1. Kinship

Let us see terms of family relation in Korean.

There are various Korean kinship terms: *sam chon* 삼촌 (father's brother), *jak eun a beo ji* 작은 아버지 (father's younger brother who married), *suk mo* 숙모 (wife of the father's or mother's younger brother), *jak eun eo meo ni* 작은 어머니 (wife of the father's younger brother), *i mo* 이모 (mother's sister), oe sam chon 외삼촌 (mother's brother), *jo ka* 조카 (nephew or niece), and so on. Even if a foreigner speaks Korean fairly well, he is always confused about those terms.

These days *chin jok* 친족 (kin) is called '*chin cheok* 친척 (relative)', '*il ga* 일가 (family)', or '*jip an* 집안 (family).' Originally, kin was divided into three sets of relatives: *bon ga* 본가 (relatives on his father's side), *oe ga* 외가 (his mother's side) and *cheo ga* 처가 (his wife's side). Because patriarchy more greatly affected Korean people after the middle of the Joseon period, the three sets covered the relatives within the eighth degree of consanguinity on one's father's side, the relatives within the fourth degree on one's mother's side, and one's wife's father and mother on her side. Generally, 'relatives' are a great-great-grandfather and his descendants who hold a memorial service for their ancestors on the father's side.

In Korea there are three types of ancestral rites still commonly performed today: *cha rye* 차례, *gi je* 기제 and *si je* 시제. First, *si je* are the rites up to two generations back on Lunar New Year's Day and the Harvest Moon Festival. Second, *gi je* are the rites held on the eve of the anniversary of the death of ancestor up to five generation back earlier in the evening, for the sake of convenience. Finally, *si je* is an annual rite held for all the ancestors of more than five generations back every October. The people who perform *si je* are called *mun jung* 문중 (clan). The clan appoints as its representative the eldest grandson in the head family of the direct descendants.

When the size of kin group is larger than that of clan, the kin group becomes part of *dong seong dong bon* 동성동본, which means people with the same surname and the same family origin. Up until just a few years ago, it was illegal for couples who had the same surname and clan name to marry, because they were descended from a common single ancestor. The law originated from a custom by which relatives on the father's side were not permitted to marry, and it was strictly observed. This is because Korean people thought that a couple with different blood ancestors have a healthy baby. Recently family law is changing with the times, as shown in the abolition of *dong seong dong bon*, because of the low birthrate and the active entry of women in public affairs.

2. Degree of consanguinity

The kinship relations in Korea are indicated by a system called *chon su* 촌수 (degree of consanguinity).

The system shows closeness or remoteness of kinship. It is thought that *chon su* has started to be used since the 12th century, which belongs to the

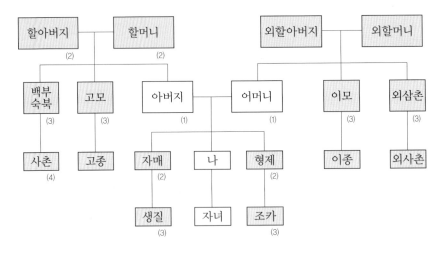

'나'를 중심으로 한 친족 계보표

Goryoe period.

Chon su is the distance between two members in the genealogy of a family represented as a rooted tree, and is defined as the degree (or number) of edges in the path between them. For example, my parents are in the first degree of consanguinity (or 1 *chon*). The distance between two members in the direct family rises one by one in proportion to the number of generation. The distance between two siblings is 2. My uncle's son is in the fourth degree (or 4 *chon*) while my brothers are in the second degree (or 2 *chon*). Further, my granduncle is in the fourth degree (or 4 *chon*) and his children are in the fifth degree (5 *chon*). In short, the even numbers 2, 4, 6 and 8 of edges in the path show that the two members are collateral relatives. On the other hand, the odd numbers 1, 3, 5 and 7 of edges in the path indicate that the upper edge and the lower edge respectively refers to my uncle and my nephew or nice. *Chon su* is also applied to the relatives on the mother's side and on the wife's side. The prefixes *oe* 외 and *cheo* 처 are respectively attached to the front of *chon su* to identify family relations on the mother's side and the wife's side, as shown in *oe sa chon* 외사촌 (the fourth degree on the mother's side) and *cheo sam chon* 처삼촌 (the third degree on the wife's side). The prefix *i* 이 refers to the mother's sisters whereas the three prefixes *baek* 백, *suk* 숙 and *go* 고 stand for the father's elder brothers, younger brothers and sisters, respectively. There is no degree of consanguinity between husband and wife because they do not have blood ties. It is said that they have nothing to do with each other once a husband and a wife are divorced although the couple lived happily together.

In Korea, distinct appellations and honorifics are assigned to families of great-great-grandchildren to great-great-grandfather. The kith and kin cover 8 *chon* on the father's side, and ancestral rites enable kindred people to keep in contact with one another. When opportunities to meet one another are decreased by an estranged blood relationship due to *chon su* going beyond the degree of consanguinity, they do not count the degree any more.

Korea's *chon su* and appellations are characteristics of Korean families which cannot be found in any other countries in the world. Also, they can be called ingenious family cultures. Only the side of relatives are indicated in China, which like Korea belongs to Asia. In other words, the Chinese prefixes *tang* 堂 and *biao* 表 stands for relatives on the father's side and the mother's side, respectively. For example, *tang ge* 堂哥 are elders who are in the fourth degree of consanguinity (4 *chon*), the sixth degree (6 *chon*) or the eighth degree (8 *chon*), and so the degree cannot be figured out. English appellations are used without distinction of sex.

3. *Dol lim ja*

Most of Korean names consist of three syllables.

The first syllable is a family name followed by a two-syllable given name that have derived from Chinese characters. Korean people are very careful in naming a baby. In particular, Joseon's Confucian patriarchal system did not permit them to name a baby boy carelessly. This is because in a given name they put '*dol lim ja* 돌림자 (circulating letters)' which indicates *chon su* (degree of consanguinity) and *hang lyeol* 항렬 (generation). *Dol lim ja* shows a person what generation level he is in.

Sons were the important workforce of the traditional Korean rural society. Korean people tried to have more sons under the influence of the patriarchal system. Someone had ten sons and there was at least a 20 year age gap or more between the eldest son and the youngest son. In the old days, it could be said that a woman and her mother-in-law gave birth to a child at the same time. Although a person was the same age as his uncle, the uncle was in the same generation level as his father's. Let me give an example. There are a man named Sang-Gyu Park and his son named Geon-Jong Park. Here, 'Sang' and 'Jong' stand for *dol lim ja* (circulating letters). 'Sang' is put in the given name of the father's brothers because they are in the same generation level as the father's. On the other hand, 'Jong' is put in the given name of the son's brothers or relatives in the fourth degree (or 4 *chon*) or the sixth degree (or 6 *chon*), as shown in 'Ho-Jong Park' and 'Myeon-Jong Park.' I should extend a person every courtesy as a superior while using honorifics towards the person, greeting him first and giving him a seat of honor, if the same *dol lim ja* as my father's is put in the person's given name although I am the same age as him. This was one of Korea's social norms.

So, *dol lim ja* can be called a very elaborate, scientific mechanism used as a way to bind a family community together, establish the order of rank in the community and observe the proprieties. Also, *dol lim ja* is one of Korea's ingenious family cultures which prevent marriages between children and their close relatives to achieve prosperity of families and their descendents.

But, the culture keeps disappearing because there is an increase in families that have one child. Recently, there is a rise in families that give a baby a given name consisting of native Korean words that cannot be written in Chinese characters. Some families name a child after his or her baptismal name under the influence of Christianity. The natural breakdown of *dol lim ja* symbolizes the weakening of the norms of courtesy in Korean society. This breakdown has the positive aspect to give children a sense of equality that transcends age or rank. But, many of the older generation worry that Korean society may become ruder day by day. So, some conservative families ask others about their family name or genealogy as a way of tracing their ancestry to judge them by the content of their character.

4. Family name and *jok bo*

All Korean people have a family name, a clan name and a given name.

A family name and a clan name tell about a person's family, and a given name, in particular *dol lim ja*, indicates what generation level he is in. When

The family tree of Park of Milseong (Miryang) clan

Korean people meet a person for the first time, they introduce themselves to him by telling him their name or hometown. If two people share a family name and a clan name, their remote ancestors are members of a family.

Korean family names show Korean people's paternal line. In Korea there are about 360 family names written in Chinese characters. The most common Korean family name is Kim, followed by Lee and Park. People who share a family name are not necessarily members of a family. The combination of a family name and a clan name indicates people's kinship. *bon gwan* 본관 (clan name) refers to birthplace of the progenitor of each clan. That is to say, a person's clan name means his ancestral home. When two people share a clan name and a family name, such as Kimhae KIm or Andong Kim, they have the same lineage. Clans were divided into various pa 파 (branches) as time went on and the number of descendants increased. For example, 'the nineteenth generation descendant of Grand Prince Yangnyeong Branch, Jeonju Lee' means a person with the family name Lee whose clan name is Jeonju and who is the nineteenth generation descendant of Grand Prince Yangnyeong.

Korean people take pride in their family names which symbolize their line of descent that have continued for hundreds or thousands of years. They took it as an unbearable insult to say what spoils their family name. So, they considered as a great disgrace the fact that they were forced to change their names to Japanese ones during the Japanese colonial era. *Dong seong dong bon* 동성동본, which literally means people with the same surname and the same family origin, were not permitted to marry because they were descended from a common single ancestor. When couples asked their consent to the marriage, whether or not they have a noble family name was an important precondition for it. The clan 'Andong Kim' in Andong district of Gyeongsangbuk-do is still called the most conservative family in Korea.

Korean people have enjoyed compiling a genealogy since the middle of the Joseon period. It is called *jok bo* 족보 in Korean. Jok bo contains the family history of the progenitor and his descendants. Most of Korean people have their *jok bo* passed down through generations. *Jok bo* does not only enable them to trace their lineages and identify their kinship relations, but it also motivates them to study harder for the honor of their family. Most Korean women's *dol lim ja* was not put in their given name because their name was scratched out of from their father's *jok bo* and then recorded on their husband's one after marriage. It is notable that Korean women keep their family name after they get married.

Korean families are spread out all over the city in the modern industrial society. Generally, Korean people do not discriminate between boys and girls but they have one or two children. So, the significance of kinship concepts, such as family name and *jok bo*, is greatly being overlooked. In particular, they could follow their mother's clan name and family name rather than taking their father's according to long tradition not until the patriarchal family system was recently abolished.

None the less, Korean people have kept family boding and kinship relations framework relatively well contrary to people of other countries. They try to revive the wealth of tradition and wisdom handed down as a family norm, give a taste of home to modern people living in isolation in mechanical civilization and inherit the spirit of mutual respect among family members. It is not too much to say that popular Korean television dramas and songs made the 'Korean Wave' because of the characteristics of Korean families and their cultures shown in these dramas and songs.

5. Greeting manners

Korean people emphasize greeting manners in addition to appellations.

Korean people think that it is rude to give a half-hearted greeting. They do not just say 'An Nyeong Ha Se Yo? (Hello!).' According to traditional Korean manners, they should use body language with speech showing respect towards elders. In the old days, Korean people did not say hello but gave a deep bow when they met a person. Here, the deep bow shows more respect towards the person. Korean greeting manners are as follows:

- *Gong su* 공수: It means putting one hand on the other hand. Korean people put their hands together when they adopt a polite attitude towards elders or attend a ceremony.
- *Mok rye* 목례: It means giving a nod. Korean people give a nod to the elder when they pass him or her by or when they get in or off an elevator.
- *Jeol* 절: It means making a bow. Korean people make a bow when they are sitting on the floor.

When Korean people meet the elder outside, they enter a room to give a deep bow to him. In Korea there are two types of bows: *pyeong jeol* 평절 (normal bow) and *keun jeol* 큰절 (deep bow). First of all, *pyeong jeol* stands for a bow made when people greet each other with the usual exchange of civilities or greet to elders on Lunar New Year's Holiday. Then, *keun jeol* refers to a deep bow made solemnly when ceremonies such as wedding and ancestral rites are performed. In this case, men and women make two and four deep bows, respectively.

Dol, Wedding Ceremony, *Hoe gap* and Ancestral Rites

1. Ceremonies of birth

In Korea, it is traditional to eat seaweed soup in the morning of one's birthday.

The tradition came from Korea's birth custom. *Dol* 돌 (first birthday) is celebrated when a baby reaches one year in age. Anyone undergoes rites of passage, such as ceremonies of *dol* and wedding and funeral rites, throughout his life. In South Korea, there are 'family rites', which consist of 'the four ceremonial occasions' of coming of age, wedding, funeral and ancestral rites and ceremonies of birth and sixtieth birthday. These family rites are still performed. They were greatly influenced by Confucianism in the Joseon kingdom. All of them focus on prosperity of descendants and ancestor worship, based on filial duty. Because they are observed by the lunar calendar, the solar dates of them are changed every year. These days many of young people celebrate their birthday by the solar calendar, but the old generation still tend to use the lunar calendar.

The infant mortality rate was high in the past when medicine was not advanced. Because Korean women had a large duty to give birth to a son to carry on their husband's family line, they laid emphasis on ceremonies of birth for prosperity of descendants. They had a custom of praying to '*sam*

The table of first-birthday party and objects for dol jab i (the ceremony of first-birthday)

shin hal meom' 삼신할멈 for them to have a son. They believed sam shin hal meom to be the goddess of childbirth. Further, they believed that a new-born baby's hip is black and blue (a Mongolian blue spot) because sam shin hal meom spanked the baby on the hip to quickly give him a start in life.

There is a custom that as a token of thanks about helping the mother give a birth to a baby, boiled rice and seaweed soup are first offered to sam shin hal meom and then the mother eats the offering. The celebrations of *sam chil il* 삼칠일 (a baby's twenty-first day of life) last for 21 days. So, Korean people call their birthday a day to eat seaweed soup.

When a woman gave birth to a baby, Korean people hang a straw rope on top of the front door to ward off evil spirits. This ceremony last for 21 days. It was good form to visit the baby not until then. The custom was derived from the belief that they should rely on the absolute thing to prevent unhappiness beyond human capabilities from arising.

When the baby reaches one year in age, a special table is laid in celebration of the baby's dol in the sense that people are sure he or she will be healthy. The table is laden with foods including *baek seol gi* 백설기 (steamed white rice cake), *su su gyeong dan* 수수경단 (honey cake made of glutinous kaoliang), *song pyeon* 송편 (rice cake steamed on a layer of pine needles), *guk su* 국수 (noodles) and various fruits. Each of these foods has a special meaning. First, *baek seol gi* means a clean mind. Second, *su su gyeong dan* is to escape from a bad luck. Third, *song pyeon* symbolizes the blessing of having things to eat. Fourth, *guk su* is to wish for a long life. Finally, jujube and fruits give a blessing over prosperity of descendents like an abundance of fruit.

The climax of dol is the ceremony '*dol jab i* 돌잡이.' During the ceremony, the boy sits before a set of objects such as money, an arrow and a writing brush, and is encouraged to grab one of them. The first object the boy picks up is believed to be a clue to the boy's culture. Money means wealth, a brush a scholar and an arrow a military officer. On the other hand, the girl sits before a set of objects, such as a ruler, colored paper and thread because needlework is considered as the greatest of the womanly virtues.

Children are dressed in traditional Korean clothes on their dol. Boys are dressed in *saek dong jeo go ri* 색동저고리 (jacket with rainbow striped sleeves), a vest, a topcoat and a hood decorated with lucky symbols stamped in gold leaf. Girls are also dressed in *saek dong jeo go ri*, a skirt and a hat. Generally, the invited guests give the child a gold ring as a gift to wish the child a long and happy life.

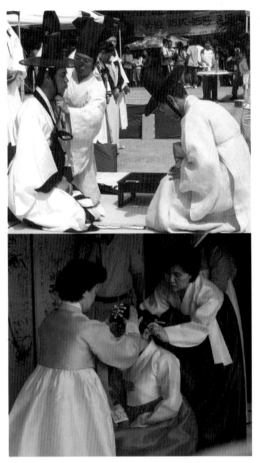

Gwan rye
Gye rye

2. Coming-up-age ceremonies

In Korea, there were two types of coming-up-age ceremonies: *gwan rye* 관례 and gye rye 계례.

Gwan rye is a ceremony where men tie up *sang tu* 상투 (a topknot), are in full dress, learn drinking manners and are given a pseudonym. Early marriage took place in the Joseon kingdom. In those days, gwan rye was performed when boys reached 12 or 13 years in age. *Gyeo rye* is a ceremony where women wear *bi nyeo* 비녀 (an ornamental hairpin) in their hair. A hair style was a symbol of adulthood in traditional Korea society. Unmarried men and women wore their hair in a long braid, but they put up their hair after the coming-up-age ceremony.

Today men and women do not wear their hair long as people did in the Joseon period and are losing interest in coming-up-age ceremonies. However, these ceremonies are still necessary. In order to congratulate all people who have reached 20 years in age over the past year, 'Coming of Age Day' was established in 1984, to be held on the third Monday in May every year. Only applicants who registered with the related organizations or institutions participate in the ceremony. It is said that being discharged from the army is the same as finishing the coming-up-age ceremony.

3. Wedding ceremony

Since the old days, it has been said that marriage is '*in ryun ji dae sa* 인륜지대사 (a major life event).'

This is because marriage is a ceremony important to individuals or families. According to Korean wedding tradition, marriage was a union of two families. In the Joseon period, it was a tendency for parents to choose marriage partners for their children after comparing their family with those of the partners rather than for parents to consent to the marriage made between their child and his or her partner who met and fell in love with each other in the natural course of their lives. So, parents consulted *jung mae jaeng i* 중매쟁이 (marriage broker) to choose marriage partners when their son(s) and daughter(s) respectively reached about 12 and 16 in age.

The custom of arranged marriage were derived from the Confucian idea of differences between the sexes which prohibits strictly that a man and a woman see each other or get together after they reached 7 years in age, as shown in '*nam nyeo chil se bu dong seok* 남녀칠세부동석 (a boy and a girl should not sit together after they have reached the age of seven).' Young people did not have any opportunities to date each other and marriage partners were chosen by their parents through marriage brokers or by seeing each other with a view to marriage. When there were talks of a marriage between two families, parents exchanged their children's *sa ju* 사주 (four pairs of cyclical characters), which literally means 'four pillars', each other.

The word *sa ju* means the year, month, day and hour of one's birth. In the East, these four elements were called four pillars which influence one's destiny. Based on *sa ju, gung hap* 궁합 (marital harmony between a man and a woman intending to marry) was predicted by fortunetellers. When the couples were blessed with good fortune and compatible with each other as marriage partners, the bride's family chose an auspicious day for a wedding ceremony. A fortuneteller ask their Chinese zodiac sign when he is consulted to check people's sa ju. Chinse zodiac signs symbolize 12 animals and are used to judge a person's character and tell fortunes. The twelve zodiacal animals are *ja* 자 (rat), *chuk* 축 (ox), *in* 인 (tiger), *myo* 묘 (rabbit), *jin* 진 (dragon), *sa* 사 (snake), *o* 오 (horse), *mi* 미 (sheep), *shin* 신 (monkey), *yu* 유 (rooster), *sul* 술 (dog), and *hae* 해 (pig). Sometimes Korean people ask people's Chinese zodiac sign rather their age when they meet for the first time.

A few days before a wedding, the groom's family sent a box for bridal gifts to the bride's house. The box is called

12 Animals symbolizing Chinese zodiac

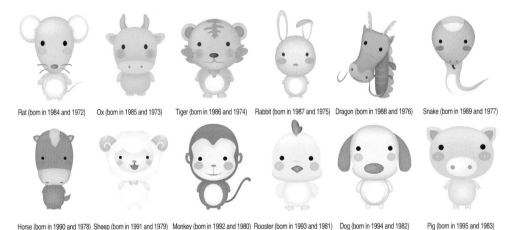

Rat (born in 1984 and 1972)　Ox (born in 1985 and 1973)　Tiger (born in 1986 and 1974)　Rabbit (born in 1987 and 1975)　Dragon (born in 1988 and 1976)　Snake (born in 1989 and 1977)

Horse (born in 1990 and 1978)　Sheep (born in 1991 and 1979)　Monkey (born in 1992 and 1980)　Rooster (born in 1993 and 1981)　Dog (born in 1994 and 1982)　Pig (born in 1995 and 1983)

'함 *ham*' and contained '*hon seo* 혼서 (marriage paper)', which specified the groom's family and the proposal of marriage, bolts of cloth and jewelry. The person who delivered the box was called '*ham jin a bi* 함진애비.' The deliverer ham jin a bi turned the ceremony into a fun and often raucous occasion. He haggled for more and asked for a sum for each step he took, shouting '*ham sa se yo* 함 사세요 (box for sale)!' as he approached the bride's house. The custom has been passed down to this day. Sometimes, I hear people shouting '*ham sa se yo!*' This reminds me of Korean wedding traditions although I am a prosaic person living in an apartment in a soulless city.

A couple of wild geese representing conjugal harmony

Traditional Korean weddings took place in the bride's home. To marry is translated into Korean as '*jang ga ga da* 장가가다', which literally means that the groom goes to the bride's house to take a wife. On the

Traditional Korean wedding ceremony

day of the wedding, the bride and groom bow to each other and share a cup of wine. The groom wore the official's uniform in the Joseon period. The bride wore *weon sam* 원삼 (a ceremonial topcoat for women with long and very wide striped sleeves), *jok du ri* 족두리 (an ornamental crown) on her head, an*d yeon ji* 연지 and *gon ji* 곤지 (rouge) on her cheeks and forehead. On the wedding night, the bride waited for the groom in '*shin bang* 신방 (the bridal room)' prepared by the bride's family. There was an interesting custom that the families of the bride and groom peeped into the bedroom of a newly married couple on the wedding night. In the old days, many women married male children who are called '*kko ma shin rang* 꼬마신랑 (child groom)' in Korean because marriages were made between couples who were chosen by their parents. It has been said that the custom was derived from the fact that people worried that the bride disappointed in the child groom would run away from the bedroom.

The bride rode in *ga ma* 가마 (palanquin) to go to the groom's house three days after the wedding ceremony. This is called '*shi jip ga da* 시집가다', which literally means that the bride goes to the groom's house to become his wife. The groom's family had a cheerful party for the bride. Then, she bowed and gave them wedding gifts from her family. In those days, women rarely visited their parent's house after their marriage, as shown in 'Be buried in the husband's home after marriage!'

Modern Korean wedding customs are greatly different form its traditional ones, under the influence of Western cultures. Most of Korean people marry for love. The groom wears a suit or tuxedo and the bride wears a white wedding dress, in stead of traditional Korean clothes. The wedding ceremony is carried out in a church or a special wedding hall other than the bride's house. The ceremony is generally performed within less than one hour. After the ceremony, a newly married couple go on a honeymoon. They invite their friends to their housewarming party in marriage acknowledgement after the honeymoon.

Today, the procedures of wedding ceremony have been simplified. But, there remain traditional Korean marriage customs, such as *ham* 함 and *pye baek* 폐백. The ceremony pye baek is an event where the newlywed couple dress into traditional Korean wedding clothes and greet their families in the wedding hall. There is also the custom that the bride buys household goods and the groom gets a house.

4. *Hoe gap*

The sixtieth birthday is called *hoe gap* 회갑 or *hwan gap* 환갑.

In old times the sixtieth birthday was a blessing because Korean people had a shorter average life. The sixtieth birthday party derived from that fact children invited their relatives to the party celebrating their parents' health and long life. A person who reached 60 years in age were well dressed and sit at a table filled with special foods prepared by their children and grandchildren. From all of them in order of age, he received bows and offerings of wine for his heath and long life. Today the significance of hoe gap has been overlooked because most of people live beyond 60.

5. Funeral and ancestral rites

A newly-married foreign woman asked me about her Korean husband.

'My husband said he would sleep over at the house of mourning. What does it mean?'

She could not understand why her husband stayed a few nights at the house of his fellow worker's family in mourning.

The Korean movie 'Festival' (1996) was set in a mourner's house in South Korea. Foreign viewers in the movie said that Korean families and traditional Korean funeral culture were very impressive. But, they wondered about why people are noisy and play *hwa tu* 화투 (flower cards) in the mourner's house. Very few people in other countries spend days together to mourn over one's death like Korean people. In Korea, funeral and ancestral rites are much more complicated than birthday parties and wedding ceremonies. This was derived from social values emphasizing the importance of filial piety.

A funeral rite is an event where people pray for the repose of the deceased. Korean people are with their parent when he or she passes away. If they do not close the eyes of his father or mother, they regret it through their life because they think it is undutiful thing. When one parent dies, *bu go* 부고 (obituary notice) is sent to people who are close to the deceased and his or her family. Leaving aside their busy schedule, these people go to offer their condolences to the family. In particular, *sang ju* 상주 (the master of a funeral rite) receives condolers and wails without sleeping before the funeral is held. The condolers do not only mourn over the death but also

Visiting to one's ancestral graves on the occasion of Chuseok

console the bereaved family. It can be said that the condolers help the chief mourner to sublimate his sadness by playiing *hwa tu* 화투 (flower cards) and to keep awake while sitting up all night with him.

In the old days funerals were held at the deceased's house. On the other hand, today many of them were held at hospital funeral halls by reasons such as a change of housing culture into apartment dwelling and convenience of condolers. Korean funeral rites are greatly simplified. For example, mourning clothes were changed from one made out of coarse hemp to a black suit and funerals generally last three days. Further, the bereaved family left off mourning on the 100th day. Those who received the obituary notice attend the funeral and give the family *bu eu geum* 부의금 (condolence money). Bu eu geum is one of Korean customs of mutual help which have been handed down for a long time. Condolers offer envelopes of money to help the family pay for the funeral expenses. This means that condolers hope the bereaved family will overcome the sorrow. So, the family remember those condolers to return a favor at their family events in the future.

Ancestral rites are events held for the spirits of the ancestors. Korean people thought that with all their heart and soul, people should honor their ancestors for the prosperity of their descendants because the spirit of those ancestors live in this world although they are the dead.

There are three types of ancestral rites: *gi je* 기제, *cha rye* 차례 and *si je* 시제. *Gi je* are ancestral rites held on the eve of *gi il* 기일 (the anniversary of the death of an ancestor). *Gi je* were performed at midnight (12 A.M.) so that they could honor the deceased for 24 hours. *Gi je* were held for all the ancestors up to five generations back, but nowadays they are performed for all the ancestors up to two generations back.

Je ju 제주 (the master of ancestral rites) places *shin wi* 신위 (memorial tablet) at the center of the ritual table. Second, *je ju* burns incense and offers wine to the dead. Finally, *je ju* makes two bows in the sense of saying good-bye to the dead. Female family members lay a table with special offerings of food and wine set in a prescribed order whereas male family members perform *gi je*. The family members share the offerings with one another after *gi je* finished. Korean people have a memory that on the day of their neighbor's *gi je* they tried to rub sleep out of their eyes expecting 'delicious foods' in their childhood when they do not have enough food for themselves.

Cha rye are the rites held in the morning on holidays such as *seol nal* 설날 (Lunar New Year's Day) and *chu seok* 추석 (Harvest Moon Festival). First of all, *seol nal* is an event where people give greetings to their ancestors for the New Year. Then, *chu seok* is a harvest festival celebrated on the 15th day of August of the lunar calendar. On *chu seok*, Korean people offer the year's harvest to their ancestors to give thanks to the ancestors. *Si je* is an annual rite held for all the ancestors of more than five generations back and is held on October of the lunar calendar. Korean people trim plants and clean the area around their ancestors' grave. *Si je* can be performed by all of the family members. Korean men tend to visit their ancestors' grave once a year no matter how busy they are. There are still many people who visit their ancestors' grave to pay their respects before they hold an important event. So, Korean people's subconscious considerably bears the respect for ancestors although South Korea is an information-oriented society.

Exercises

01 Read the following explanations. If they are right, put O in the
brackets next to them. If they are wrong, put X instead.
1) One of characteristics of Korean traditional families is a patriarchal
family system. (   )
2) There are seats in the subways and buses of South Korea that are
designated as seats for seniors. (   )
3) *Chon su* is a system indicating the kinship relations in Korea. (   )
4) Korean women take their husband's family name after they get
married. (   )
5) Gi je are ancestral rites honoring ancestors and held at night. (   )

02 Korean people are very careful in naming a baby. In particular,
they named a baby boy carefully and why? But, today the custom
is changing and why?

03 What are the most three common family names in Korea?

04 What are traditional Korean wedding customs still commonly
observed today?

05 What are characteristics of Korean families and give an example
of each characteristic.

Korean People Who Say 'The Tailor Makes the Man.'

Step 1 Korean People and Clothes

There is a Korean proverb which says '*The Tailor Makes the Man.* 옷이 날개 (Clothes make the man).'

The proverb means that well-dressed people look better and shows Korea people's subconsciousness which bears an emphasis on clothing. Korean people think that clothes can tell about one's personality and culture.

For Korean people, 'clothing' take priority over 'food', as shown in the expression '*eu* 의 (clothing), *sik* 식 (food) and *ju* 주 (shelter).' This came from the thought that a noble man should not reveal his poverty while adjusting himself although he is too poor to have food. In old times, liege subjects adjusted their clothing to manage the affairs of state in front of the king. It was taught that one should be decently dressed before doing anything.

It was thought that clothing do not only means covering the body but they also shows the wearers' relationship manners and personality. In the past Korean women should not wear a sleeveless shirt before parents-in-law even on hot days. The family members were not at home all day in their pajamas. People put on their socks and dressed up for greeting a guest before he or she came to see them. They wear a black suit and a black necktie when going to offer their condolences to a family in mourning. So,

Korean people make an emphasis on clothing and its manners which are suitable according to time, circumstances and people they meet.

Korea has clear four seasons. Korean people change their clothes according to the season. In summer they wear cool clothes and in winter warm ones. They make or fix clothing every season. Accordingly, they became better at handling clothing and more interested in clothes. Korean people have a reputation that they dress more fashionably than people of other countries. Young Korean people are so sensitive about the trends that they enjoy wearing clothes showing their individuality. Because they avoid wearing the same clothes, they change their clothes every day. Nowadays people can purchase various types of clothes chiefly through an online shopping mall.

For the above reasons, Korea's fashion industry is famous in the world. Korean clothing products can be found anywhere in the world. Korean clothes are cheaper than French or Italian ones, but they are very excellent in design and color. They are favored in the world market because of no discoloration after washing them and Korean people's meticulous sewing skills. In South Korea there are many departments of clothing & textiles and fashion design in universities. The new generation strong on individuality is greatly interested in fashion industry occupations such as fashion designer, fashion model, internet shopping mall administrator, clothing merchandiser, fashion coordinator and fashion displayer. Andre Kim is one of the most famous fashion designer in South Korea. He held fashion shows all over the world and played a great role in the globalization of Korean fashion.

Step 2 *Han Bok* Culture

1. Characteristics of *han bok*

Han bok are traditional Korean clothes.

Han bok has been worn since the Three Kingdom period. In those days, han bok were similar to Chinese clothes. *Jeo go ri* 저고리 (traditional Korean jacket) grew shorter and *ot go reum* 옷고름 (ribbon) was attached to either side of *jeo go ri* in the Joseon period. '*Han bok*' worn in the Joseon period is the version that is used today.

It is notable that the neckband of *jeo go ri* forms a V-shape other than Chinese-style with mandarin collars and that *jeo go ri* ties at the front with *ot go reum*. There are 55 costumes of Chinese ethnic minorities at the Folk Costume Museum in Beijing, China. Only Chinese Korean costume is cut fairly low at the neck. Chinese Korean people are the descendants of those who emigrated from Korea into China during the Japanese colonial time. Today people wear Chinese-style jackets with mandarin collars in most countries which share borders with China. So, *han bok* show Korean people's creative Traditional Korean clothes for women consist of *jeo go ri* and *chi ma* 치마 (skirt). *Jeo go ri* is cut just over the breasts, and the neckband is trimmed with *dong jeong* 동정 (a thin, white and cloth-covered paper collar) to make a beautiful neckline. *Jeo go ri* is slit down the front and ties with long ot go reum attached to either side of it. *Han bok* shows elegance because of the harmonization between the curve of sleeves of *jeo go ri* and the straight line of *chi ma*. *Chi ma* is a cloth worn underneath *jeo go ri*. *Chi ma* is a wrap-around gathered skirt that has shoulder straps and is tied around the chest the top of the skirt sits. Because *chi ma* is slit at the side, it can be called 'a two-dimensional fabric.' That is to say, *chi ma* is a wrap-around barrel skirt and slit at the side without a seam. If I wear *chi ma*, I feel that it is light. *Chi ma* streaming in the wind is very feminine. *Chi mat ba ram* 치맛바람, which literally means wind of skirt, was derived from the streaming skirt. The meaning of the expression changed from the swish of a skirt to the influence of a woman's power. Nowadays, it is used in a negative sense. In the Joseon period women wore *ssu gae chi ma* 쓰개치마 (cloak) to hide face when they went out. Sometimes historical dramas in South Korea show that women wear ssu gae *chi ma*.

Traditional Korean clothes for men consist of *ba ji* 바지 (trouser) and *jeo go ri*. *Jo kki* 조끼 (vest), *ma go ja* 마고자 (outer jacket) and *du ru ma gi* 두루마기 (long coat) were worn over *jeo go ri*. *Ba ji* is so a baggy trouser that it is convenient to sit on the floor. The baggy trouser was designed to be suitable to a sedentary lifestyle. *Ba ji* is bound at the waist with *heo ri tti* 허리띠 (a strip of cloth) and at the ankles with *dae nim* 대님 (cloth bands). In the Joseon period, men wore *du ru ma gi* over ordinary clothes and *gat* 갓 (a horse hair hat) when they went out. Also, they wore *du ru ma gi* when they performed ancestral rites at home. This is because *du ru ma gi* belonged to a suit in those days.

Kinds and colors of *han bok* vary according to sex, age and status. Korean people are called 'People of the White Cloth.' This is because most of them wore white clothes. But, royal costumes and *gwan bok* 관복

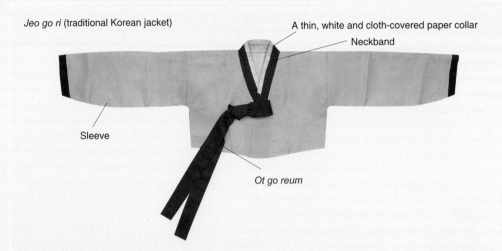

Jeo go ri (traditional Korean jacket)

A thin, white and cloth-covered paper collar

Neckband

Sleeve

Ot go reum

A woman wearing *han bok* in the picture (the Joseon period)

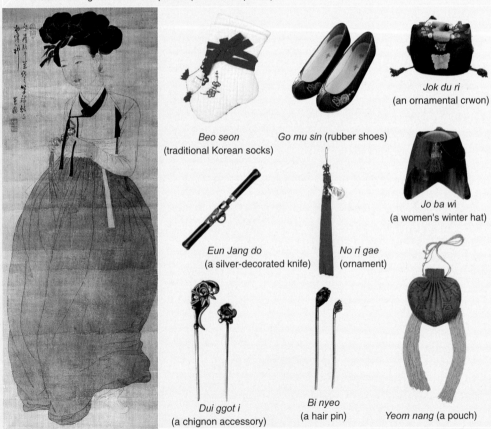

Beo seon
(traditional Korean socks)

Go mu sin (rubber shoes)

Jok du ri
(an ornamental crwon)

Eun Jang do
(a silver-decorated knife)

No ri gae
(ornament)

Jo ba wi
(a women's winter hat)

Dui ggot i
(a chignon accessory)

Bi nyeo
(a hair pin)

Yeom nang (a pouch)

102

(official uniforms) were various in color. Children wore *saek dong jeo go ri* 색동저고리 (jacket with rainbow striped sleeves). Newly-married women wore yellow green *jeo go ri* and red *chi ma*.

Han bok were made from different fabrics by season. In winter people wore silk clothes or clothes thickly padded with cotton. In summer they made their own *jeo go ri* with ramie or hemp fabric. In autumn they used soft fabric to make their clothes. The characteristic of *han bok* is as light as a feather because most fabric used to make it is generally thin and soft. So, people wearing *han bok* walk lightly.

People should put on underwears properly to wear *han bok* beautifully. They should put on layers of underskirts so as not to expose their bare skin because *chi ma* is split at the side. So, there are many underwears in *han bok*. The layers of underwears keep out the cold in winter. In winter people wearing *han bok* do not feel the cold. There is a large space between clothes. People wear accessories to wear *han bok* more beautifully. When a woman wears *han bok* with *no ri gae* 노리개 (ornament), *jok du ri* 족두리 (an ornamental crown) decorated with jewels, fastened to the head with *bi nyeo* 비녀 (hair pin), and put on *beo seon* 버선 (traditional Korean socks) and *go mu sin* 고무신 (rubber shoes), she can show traditional Korean beauty more clearly.

Han bok are wide and suit any body type. Old people hesitate to wear *qi pao* 旗袍 (Chinese dress) because they are narrow and show body line clearly. But, *han bok* do not only cover the fat on old people's stomach completely but also make them more beautiful or mature. The long curve of *chi ma* makes fat people look slim. Pleats on *chi ma* make skinny people look less thinner. So, all of Korean people have love and pride of *han bok*.

people wear *han bok*, they naturally have a courteous and obedient attitude. They behave themselves so as not to step on *chi ma* and to get their *ot go reum* wet because *chi ma* are long and wide. This shows *han*

Children's *han bok*   Adults' *han bok*

Commemorative photograph of heads of government of 21 Asia-Pacific Economic Cooperation (APEC) members wearing han bok

bok's influence on Korean people's courteous attitude. So, Korean children must wear *han bok* when they are taught traditional Korean manners.

2. Changes of *han bok*

Western clothes were introduced to Korea when its civilization came into Korea. Korean people did not wear *han bok* in their daily life as they started to put on Western clothes after Korea's independence from Japan in 1945. It is a real hassle to dress up *han bok* because they have complicated formalities and are difficult to mend. For example, women wear *chi ma*, *jeo go ri*, layers of underwears, *beo seon* and *go mu sin*. Nowadays, *han bok* are mainly not as casual clothes but as ceremonial ones for holidays or a wedding.

Nonetheless, Korean people like wearing *han bok* because of the beautiful style of dressing. This led to appearance of s*aeng hwal han bok* 생활 한복 (casual han bok). *Saeng hwal han bok* are those which were made by using traditional Korean beauty and considering practical use. That is to say, *saeng hwal han bok* are convenient to walk or work. People who wear casual *han bok* put on shoes instead of *go mu sin*.

These days a lot of ready-made *han bok* are sold in the market. There are a lot of beautiful *han bok* in shopping malls of Jongno or Dongdaemun Market in Seoul, where people can try them on to buy. In particular, *han bok* have been popular as colorful party wears among young people since a television series such as '*Dae jang geum* 대장금 (A Jewel in the Palace)' or '*Hwang jin Yi* 황진이' gained popularity. Web sites related to *han bok* supply a variety of information of them: the way to wear *han bok* beautifully and well-matched accessaries with *han bok* for sale.

Recently there are many fashion shows to introduce the beauty of *han bok* in the world. In order to globally spread awareness of *han bok, han bok* designer Young-Hee Lee chose Paris as her sphere of activity and established Museum of *Han Bok* in New York. She showed *han bok*, such as royal costumes, ordinary people's clothes, Buddhist monk's robes, traditional wedding dress and female shaman's clothes under the title '*Han bok*: Clothing of the Wind.'

Asia-Pacific Economic Cooperation (APEC) was held in South Korea in 2005. At that time, the heads of government of 21 APEC members including USA wore *du ru ma gi* to take a commemorative photograph.

Exercises

01 Read the following explanations. If they are right, put O in the brackets next to them. If they are wrong, put X instead.

1) Nowadays, *han bok* are mainly worn as ceremonial ones for holidays or a wedding. (　　)

2) Newly-married women wore red *jeo go ri* and *chi ma*. (　　)

3) Because chi ma is slit at the side, it can be called 'a two-dimensional fabric.' (　　)

4) It is considered that Korean people's courteous attitude was influenced by *han bok*. (　　)

5) In the Joseon period, men wore *du ru ma gi* over ordinary clothes and *gat* 갓 (a horse hair hat) when they went out. (　　)

02 Explain the reason why Korean people are called 'People of the White Cloth.'

03 Explain the reason why Korean children must wear *han bok* when they are taught traditional Korean manners, making connections between these manners and characteristics of *han bok*'s shape.

04 What are called *han bok* made by using traditional Korean beauty and considering practical use. Where are many of them can be found in Seoul?

05 Who is the designer that showed *han bok* under the title 'Han bok: Clothing of the Wind' so as to globally spread awareness of them. And, who is the representative fashion designer in South Korea?

Kimchi, Hot and Mouth-watering!

Step 1 Cooked Rice and Soup

1. Rice-oriented culture

'Aren't they fed up with three rice meals a day?'

Chinese students question Korean eating habits. They say it would be better if Korean people eat dumpling or noodles once a day instead of rice as Chinese people do.

Food reflects natural topography and culture of a country. Korea belongs to the rice culture area. In Korea, cooked rice is a staple food and accompanied by a soup and a variety of side dishes. Korean people's love for rice is particularly unique. Some of them say that they do not have a meal without rice even though they eat hearty *naeng myeon* 냉면 (Korean cold noodles) in summer.

There are many Korean expressions related with rice to describe significant things such as 'the number of rice bowl' and 'to lose the rice bowl' which mean 'their age' and 'to lose a job', respectively.

Korean people are sensitive to the taste of cooked rice as much as they love it. They generally like newly-cooked warm and 'glutinous' rice. The expression '*chan bab sin se* 찬밥신세', which literally means 'cold rice life', depicts the situation that a guest gets a cold reception in the sense that Korean people are served cold cooked-rice although they do not like eating

it. So, restaurants serving newly-cooked hot rice are always full of customers. It is generally said that a meal with lackluster rice was bad despite its wonderful side dishes.

This rice-based diet can cause a excessive carbohydrate consumption. From the old times, Korean people added vegetables, nuts, seafoods or meats to rice for a nutritionally balanced diet. *Gim bap* 김밥 (rice rolled in laver), *bi bim bap* 비빔밥 (rice mixed with vegetable and beef), and *o gok bap* 오곡밥 (five grain rice) for the first full moon day of the year are nutritionally balanced foods. Everyone enjoys *gim bap*, a combination of fresh vegetables and seafood because it is good for beauty as well as a light meal. *Bi bim bap* mainly consists of cooked rice and vegetables, and it contains low calories. So, it is very helpful for beauty and weight loss.

Cooked rice should be accompanied by some watery and salty foods called side dishes. So, these foods are cooked pleasantly salty. *Guk* 국, which literally means 'soup', is a basic dish for the Korean table setting and it is seasoned with salt. *Guk* is not the same with a soup. Korean people do not eat only *guk*. The cost of side dishes is not calculated separately because they are entailed with rice. When people order two servings of *bul go gi*

Gim bap and tteok

불고기, the cost for side dishes such as kimchi, *na mul* 나물 (cooked vegetables), *bu chim gae* 부침개 (vegetable pancakes), lettuce, *ssam jang* 쌈장 (a thick, spicy condiment used with food wrapped in a leaf in Korean cuisine), pieces of garlic and braised side dishes in some sauce is not charged. So these side dishes are called *mit ban chan* 밑반찬 (basic side dish). This is because additional kimchi and lettuce are served for free.

2. *Guk mul*-based diet

'It is interesting that most Korean eating utensils are concave.'

Foreigners who were affected Korean wave and watched Korean dramas say as above. While most of countries use flat dishes, Korean traditional dinnerware is concave. Korean spoons are also deep and big compared to other countries'. This shows that *guk mul* 국물 (watery food) is considered a basic dish for the Korean table setting.

Korean vocabulary also prove that *guk mul* is essential for the Korean table setting. In order of the proportion of water in food, *guk mul* is classified into *tang* 탕 (soup), *guk* 국 (soup), *jji gae* 찌개 (stew) and *jjim* 찜 (steamed dish) and the styles of *guk mul* are different from one another. In English, *guk mul* can be referred as soup or stew. In Chinese, all of them just belong to *tang* 탕 (soup). That is, *doen jang jji gae* 된장찌개 (soybean paste stew) as well as *doen jang guk* 된장국 (soybean paste soup) are a kind of *tang* and *gom guk* 곰국 (beef soup cooked with brisket, shank and intestines) is also one of *tang*.

Seol leong tang, the representative one of Korean watery foods

A variety of *guk mul* is made with vegetables put in boiling water. Korea has more abundant water resources than other countries, since its annual average precipitation is about 1300mm. As shown in the proverb, 'spend money like water', the table setting comes from the abundance of water. In addition, vegetables from mountains and fields are plentiful in Korea, because mountain area accounts for 70% of its whole territory. *Guk mul* is ideal to moisten dry throat when people eat rice. So, ordinary Korean table is fundamentally set with rice and guk.

'What food do you think when you are feeling a little hungry in cold winter?'

If you ask Korean people as above, they will answer 'a bowl of hot *guk mul*.' A hungover person would answer that he wants hot and spicy *hae jang guk* 해장국 (hangover soup). Some people would answer that they miss a bubbling and boiling soybean paste stew. Early Korean immigrants in U.S. made and ate *gal bi tang* 갈비탕 (beef rib soup), made of the part of beef rib that American didn't eat. Now, Western people enjoy *gal bi tang* and say that it makes their stomach feel better and more comfortable. A hot soup warms stomach, stimulates digestion and helps blood circulation. This is because Korean people express satisfaction with hot boiling *guk mul*, saying 'The soup was really cool' although they scald their tongue or sweat a lot.

3. Development of storable and fermented foods

People in all countries flavor foods with salt. Korean culinary culture is developed one step further compared to other countries. Korean people add saltness with '*jang* 장' (condiment), which is made by mixing salt and soybeans. *Jang* is a basic condiment for Korean food and a source of protein. It is also a healthy food ingredient made through long-time fermentation and prevents adult disease. So, Korean people have sincerely devoted to make and preserve *jang*, a basic ingredient for all food, since long before.

The process to make *jang* is as follow:

1. Boil soybeans to make fermented soybean lump.
2. Ferment the boiled soybean lumps with salt and water.

The solid ingredient is called *doen jang* 된장 named after *doe jik ha da* 되직하다 which literally means 'a bit thick.' The liquid is called *gan jang* 간장 named after *gan gan ha da* 간간하다, which literally means 'pleasantly salty'. As shown in the Korean expression 'Friends and jang improve with age', Korean people store *gan jang* 간장 (soybean sauce), *doen jang* 된장 (soybean paste), and *go chu jang* 고추장 (red pepper paste) in a big jar and use them for a long time.

Red pepper paste is made of ground red pepper and is essential for *mae un tang* 매운탕 (hot spicy fish soup)'s seasoning or for raw fish. Especially, this red pepper paste removes fish odors so that it is essential seasoning for braised fish or stew. Fishing lovers usually bring it. Korean people bring it when they go abroad to make their greasy stomach comfortable with this

Fermented soybeans, the
ingredients of soy paste

Fermented soybean being changed into soy paste in a pot

Pots containing various
fermented sauce

spicy red pepper paste. Kimchi, daily served side dish, is another preserving food through fermentation. Kimchi is made by mixing various vegetables and salt-fermented seafood. Some regard Korean food as slow food because there are many Korean food requiring long time to cook and preserving for long term.

4. Harmony of food and yak sik dong won philosophy

The Korean drama 'Dae jang geum' shows Korean traditional royal court food. In the drama, diseases are healed by balance of ingredients' *yin* 음 (negative forces) and *yang* 양 (positive forces), the harmony of food ingredients. Korean people were interested in that products from nature have a medicinal action because these natural products correspond with human body's *yin*-and-*yang* principle. The interest caused them to use vegetables and fruits from mountains and field for food ingredients as well as medicinal herbs.

The word *yang nyeom* 양념 (condiment) came from '*yak nyeom* 약념', which is a abbreviation of "*Yaki doedorok yeomdue dunda* 약이 되도록 염두에 둔다" (having condiments in mind as a medicine). This shows that green onion, garlic, ginger and ground red pepper as well as soy sauce and soybean paste can be medicines for our body.

Nowadays, with the rise in obesity, adult diseases such as diabetes, heart disease and hypertension are also increasing. However, the obesity rate in South Korea is relatively lower compared to other country because Korean food is mainly based on vegetables and contains well-balanced carbohydrates, proteins, fats and few calories. kimchi and *bi bim ba*p are already known for weight loss diet worldwide. So, *yak sik dong won* 약식동원 (food and medicine are of the same origin) philosophy is proven by the scientific evidence that Korean foods prevents from obesity and are health foods.

Step 2 Table Setting and Table Manners

1. Table setting

- In the traditional Korean table setting, all dishes are served on one table at the same time. Rice or other dishes are not served one after another during a meal.
- A rice bowl is on the left, and a soup bowl on the right side of the rice bowl. Soy sauce placed in the center of the table and other side dishes are put around the soy sauce.
- Put spoon and chopsticks next to the soup evenly.
- Put *jji gae* in the center of the table. Family members share one *jji gae*, but it is possible to prepare a small ladle to serve themselves if there is a guest.
- In the old days, people used a dishcloth to wipe the dropped food. Nowadays, napkins or table tissues are prepared.
- Drink alcohol only one or two shots during a meal. The dining table is provided with rice as a main dish. The liquor table is set if it is to drink alcohol. Due to this customs, Korean people have a meal quickly and move to a bar or pub to drink. The culture of "*cha* 차 (round)" of social activity is originated from round(s) of drinks after a meal.
- Serve water to finish a meal because the end of a meal is drinking "*sung*

nyung 숭늉(scorched-rice water)." In recent days, people usually drink mineral water or barley tea instead of sung nyung.

- Prepare refreshment table after finishing a meal. For the traditional refreshment table, *tteok* 떡 (rice cake), *su jeong gwa* 수정과 (cinnamon and dried persimmon punch), and/or *sik hye* 식혜 (saccharified rice drink) are served. Recently, instead of the separate refreshment table, people drink coffee or eat fruits at the same dining table.

- Foreigners' favorite Korean foods are *dol sot bi bim bap* 돌솥비빔밥 (rice hash cooked in a stone pot), *gim bap* 김밥 (rice rolled in laver), *mul naeng myeo*n 물냉면 (buckwheat noodles in chilled broth), *bul go gi* 불고기 (Korean barbecue), *jap chae* 잡채 (potato starch noodles stir-fried with vegetables), *sam gye tang* 삼계탕 (ginseng chicken soup), *so gal bi* 소갈비 (beef ribs), *dak gal bi* 닭갈비 (spicy, stir-fried chichen ribs), *tteok bbokk i* 떡볶이 (rice cakes in hot sauce), *sam gyeop sal gu i* 삼겹살구이 (pork belly roasting), *kimchi bokk eum bap* 김치볶음밥 (kimchi fried rice), *sut bul doe ji gal bi* 숯불돼지갈비 (charcoal-broiled spareribs), and *je yuk bokk eum* 제육볶음 (stir-fried spicy pork).

2. Table manners

In the traditional Korean table manner, whole family members eat together. When they had a meal together with elders, table for the eldest was set separately. Grandchildren could learn table manners while eating with their grandfather at the same table. Domestic upbringing was conducted through this '*bab sang meo ri* education 밥상머리 교육', where the word '*bab sang meo ri*' literally means 'the corner of the table prepared with foods.'

- Korean people use a right hand to have a meal. Do not use both hands.

- Do not hold the spoon and chopsticks together in one hand.
- At first, taste soup to moisten throat, and then try cooked rice. This is called *sul jeok sim* 술적심, which came from the expression *bab han sul* 밥 한 술, a spoon of rice. This habit is Korean ancestors' wisdom not to have an upset stomach due to dry rice.
- The traditional Korean table manners respect elderly people. When having a meal with the elderly, wait for the elders to hold their spoon first and keep pace with elders. If you finish the meal before the elderly, wait and stay calmly until they finish their meal.
- Do not hold the rice bowl or hot soup bowl in your hand during a meal. Chinese and Japanese people hold and eat their rice bowl which is much smaller than Korean bowl. It is hard to hold rather a big bowl containing newly-cooked hot rice during a meal.
- Chew food with your closed mouth and do not make noises while chewing. When coughing or sneezing during a meal, face the other way from the table and cover your mouth with your hand or napkin.
- In the old days, Korean people educated their children, as follows: "Have a meal just and quietly!" or "If you shake your leg, you will lose your luck when having a meal." They had conversation at the refreshment table after finishing the meal. Men often have conversation for a long time at the liquor table instead of the refreshment table.
- Korean people tend to eat faster than other countries' people since they eat without talking. Some people say that the tendency results from Korean people's hot temper. But it is caused by many hot dishes and sedentary lifestyle. In the old days, Korean people placed a low table on the floor for a meal. The reason why Korean people did not talking during a meal is to prevent the situation spilling hot soup by hitting the bowl with a spoon and to have a meal carefully. In the same vein, they taught their children not to shake their leg because dishes could be spilt

by hitting the leg of the low table with the shaking leg. Moreover, as all dishes are served on one table at the same time, Korean people needed to eat them before they are cooled down. Warm food is better to digest and more delicious. Chinese and Western people are talking while waiting for next dishes because all of dishes are served one after another consecutively. Today Korean table manners are changing to have a conversation and eat slowly like Chinese and Western people because they have a meal sitting on a chair which does not cause pins and needles in their leg.

• Those who asked for having a meal or an elder person pays for the meal. It is still strange for Korean people to pay their bills separately.

3. Korean tableware, spoon and chopsticks

Korean people use a spoon a lot.

There are many watery foods and *bi bim bap* eaten with a spoon in Korea. Spoons are used to scoop cooked rice or to mix cooked rice with vegetables to make *bi bim bap*. The manner of spoon was strict. For example, in the family the biggest and best spoon is given to the father to distinguish it from other members'. The first table manner taught children is to place a spoon evenly.

"I can't believe Korean people share one bowl of soybean paste stew all together?"

Even a foreigner who fairly adjusts to Korean culture is overwhelmed by sharing soups from one bowl.

Korean people believe that from a perspective of blood ties, it is natural for '*hansotbapeul meoknun sikgu* 한솥밥을 먹는 식구 (family members who live under the same roof)' to share food from one bowl and that the sharing makes the family members feel closer to one another. This belief is based

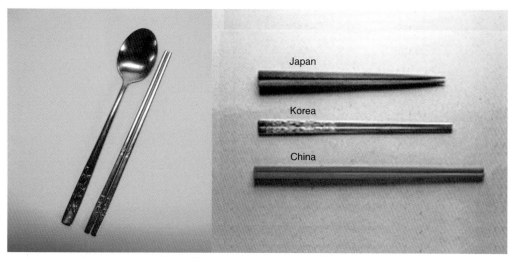

Korean spoon and chopsticks   Chopsticks in Korea, China and Japan

on emotional idea, not on a sense of hygiene. Korea early introduced an agrarian society in which all villagers were relatives and did not feel any tension and pressure. In recent years, it is a hygienic table manner to use an individual plate for one's own food and not to put his or her spoon into the bowl or platter for entire table during business meals. Sharing *jji gae* from one bowl and giving delicious parts of fish to others help to make a closer relationship and to show consideration like a family, though. Korean people's sharing food from one bowl is the symbol of closeness. Respect to the sense of hygiene, restaurants provide a separate plate and a small ladle. But, in regular family meals, they think soybean paste stew tastes more delicious when they scoop it from one earthen pot all together

Korean people mainly use metal chopsticks, not wooden ones.

Foreigners say that metal chopsticks are offensive when the chopsticks touch their mouth. Those who are not accustomed to using chopsticks can eat food more easily with wooden ones than metal ones. This is because wooden chopsticks do not slip easily in their hand. Otherwise, merits of

Correct spoon grip

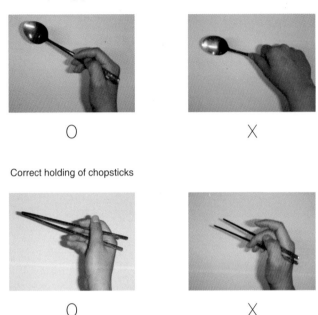

O   X

Correct holding of chopsticks

O   X

metal chopsticks are that it is possible to pick up foods exactly with them and that foods rarely slip down between these chopsticks. There are so many Korean braised vegetable foods. The preference of foods makes it difficult to use wooden chopsticks. For instance, wooden chopsticks are easy to be broken when a big radish speared by them. In addition, watery foods are common in Korean foods which cause discoloration or twisting to wooden ones. Brazen utensil and silver spoon not only notify agricultural chemicals by changing their color to black but also kill harmful bacteria.

Culinary culture is different by the shape of chopsticks even among Korea, China and Japan where chopsticks are mainly used to pick up foods. Chinese chopsticks are longer and more squarish and Japanese ones are shorter and thinner. Japanese ones are suitable to lift rice or noodle to mouth and to debone the small, delicate pieces of fish bones. Korean ones are of middle size and made of metal other than wooden.

Nowadays, culinary culture has been greatly changed. One of the changes is an appearance of kitchen scissors on the table. Kitchen scissors play an important role in picking up or tearing some food at home as well as at the restaurant, instead of chopsticks. It is presumed that an increase in meat consumption by economic growth in Korea results in introducing the use of kitchen scissors. Eating *bul go gi* 불고기 and pork on the grill has been common, and scissors are more convenient to cut meat than chopsticks.

Step 3 Kimchi and *Mak geol li*

1. Kimchi, fermented food

Kimchi is a vegetable side dish by which cooked rice is accompanied.

There are more big fans of kimchi in foreign countries than expected. These fans say one's mouth water whenever he hears the word 'kimchi' once he eats kimchi three times. The hot taste of kimchi stimulates people's taste buds which cause them to want to eat kimchi continuously. Unlike salads, kimchi is too hot to eat alone. It is required to eat kimchi during a meal.

Kimchi is a fermented food made of brined vegetables with a variety salt-fermented seafoods and seasonings. There are hundreds of varieties of kimchi in accordance with a main vegetable ingredient, even more than cheeses in France. Almost all vegetables can be a main ingredient of kimchi. *Dong chi mi* 동치미 (white and chilled watery radish kimchi) and *kkak du gi* 깍두기 (diced radish kimchi) are made of radishes. *Geot jeo ri* 겉절이 (fresh vegetable salad with kimchi seasoning) is made of cucumbers, green onions, leeks and pepper leaves. Korean people say '*dam geu da* 담그다' which means 'to make' kimchi or soybean paste. This word is involved with 'mature, ripening and fermented' to express making of fermented food. Kimchi has its unique sour smell caused by the effect of

People doing gim jang

lactobacillus several days later after it was made. This sour kimchi is helpful to prevent constipation and adult diseases as well as has a anti-cancer effect. Kimchi is a healthy food containing abundant lactobacillus, vegetable alkaline, and dietary fiber to make up for the acidifying diet of modern people. Vitamin C contained in red pepper used as an ingredient of kimchi is 50 times richer than that contained in apple. Foreign female tourists are increasing due to kimchi's effectiveness on skin care and weigh loss.

Even over-fermented kimchi is not thrown away. It is used to cook a lot of dishes such as kimchi *jji gae* 김치찌개 (Kimchi stew), kimchi *bokk eum bap* 김치볶음밥 (kimchi fried rice), kimchi *jeon* 김치전 (kimchi pancake), kimchi *ramen* 김치라면, *yeol mu* kimchi *naeng myeon* 열무김치 냉면 (cold noodle with young summer radish kimchi) and *du bu* kimchi 두부김치 (stir-fried tofu and kimchi). Kimchi can be also used in foreign foods. For example, Chinese food can be a excellent food when fried with over-fermented kimchi and pork together. Fried rice with chopped up kimchi is spicy and not greasy so that it is very delicious. If we eat dumpling with *mul* kimchi 물김치 (watery kimchi), it goes down nicely. Kimchi is combined with greasy foods such as pizza and burger to reduce oily taste and add to improve its flavor. Now, fusion foods customized to Western tastes are being developed, for instance, kimchi sandwich and kimchi spaghetti.

Korean people eat kimchi everyday as they feel other side dishes are not needed if they have kimchi. They are never run out of kimchi in their refrigerator. it is possible to make kimchi at anytime because napa cabbage is available for all year around. In the past, autumn is the time for making kimchi with more than 100 heads of newly harvested napa cabbage to store up and save kimchi for the winter. This preparation of large quantities of kimchi for the winter is called '*gim jang* 김장.' *Gim jang* was an important family event to provide them with nutrition throughout winter and it was shared by families, relatives and neighbors. The traditional way to preserve kimchi in a good condition in winter is to store kimchi in earthenware jars in the ground. After South Korean people began to live in the apartment, they keep kimchi in the fridge instead of burying kimchi jars in the ground. Many Korean preserved foods such as kimchi cause South Korean people to use a rather big fridge than people in other countries. 'Kimchi fridge 김치냉장고 (a dedicated fridge for kimchi)' has been developed and loved by a lot of families. As the number of working women has been increased, the types of kimchi sold in the market have been diversifying. Portable kimchi and small package kimchi are common and various kinds of them can be purchased.

2. *Bul go gi* and *ssam*

With Kimchi, *bul go gi* is the representative Korean food recognized worldwide. *Bul go gi* is a dish grilled of thinly sliced beef that is pre-marinated with various seasonings to enhance its flavor and tenderness. It is the most loved Korean food by foreigners. It is an appropriate food for social gathering because people can enjoy seeing the beef cooked on the charcoal grill and having a friendly conversation while it is being done.

The secret of *bul go gi* is sauce. Any greasy beef has

Bul gogi

good and deep flavor without greasy taste if it is marinated with various seasoning. Seasoning sauce of *bul go gi* consists of soy sauce, sugar, minced garlic, minced green onion, sesame salt, ground black pepper, sesame oil, etc. The taste of *bul go gi* varies by the amount and proportion of each ingredients. Thinly sliced beef is marinated with the sauce for one day. Then, the marinated beef is barbecued on the charcoal grill to eat instantly. The barbecued beef, *bul go gi*, is served with lettuce, perilla leaf or other leafy vegetable which are used to wrap a slice of the meat. Pine mushroom, matsutake, or pine leaf is sometimes grilled with the beef to give flavor. Besides *bul go gi*, Korean people like to grill and eat meat themselves, because it stimulates their appetite.

It is nutritious and delicious to eat meat with vegetables. Barbecued *bul go gi*, beef or pork on the charcoal grill is more delicious when wrapped in fresh vegetables. This Korean cuisine, wrapping meat in leafy vegetables, is called *ssam* 쌈. Acid in meat and alkaline in vegetable are balanced by this eating habit. The recipe of *ssam* is as follow. (1) Wash your hands. (2) Spread a leaf of lettuce on your left palm. (3) Put a piece of meat on the lettuce accompanying *ssam jang* 쌈장 (condiment), garlic, or green pepper. (4) Wrap them in a bite-size. South Korean people make and give *ssam* each other with their warm heart.

3. Drinking culture of Korea

In South Korea the most strange thing to foreigners is drinking culture of Korea.

"Why do Korean people drink so immoderately until Round 2 or 3?

In a word, Korean men are reputed a 'heavy drinker.' They say 'who don't drink alcohol is not a man' or 'poor drinker can not get ahead in the world.' These reflect that in a Korean society people are inwardly plied with liquor and enjoy treating others to a drink. But, bringe drinking does not necessarily represent Korean traditional drinking culture.

Korean ancestors enjoyed drinking as an art to thank mother nature and to enjoy their life. They brewed alcoholic beverages every season and appreciated the beauty of life with a dear guest and the fine drinks. They matched each drink with the suitable food for their health and drink moderately. For example, *mak geol li* 막걸리 (the traditional korean drink) has low alcohol content.

Korean people believe drinking etiquettes to be important from old times. When people reach to a certain age to drink alcohol, Korean ancestors forced them to have their first drink in front of elders in order not to have bad drinking habits. Drinking etiquettes are taught sons by fathers, and pupils by elders. According to traditional Korean drinking etiquettes, people can drink alcohol with permission from elders. So, they do not decline a glass of alcohol given from elders. When elders give a glass of alcoholic drink to youngers, youngers should receive it politely. When drinking in front of elders, youngers turn their body. It means refraining from drinking liquor indiscreetly before elders. Also it is a polite manner to pour drinks elders and superior first.

"Why do Korean people pass their glass to others?"

Most of Western people think Korean 'passing a glass around' unhygienic. This is an unique Korean drinking culture. The practice originated from the custom that when the host of memorial service for his ancestor offers relatives to partake of sacrificial drink, the receiver drinks it and passes it to the host. This passing is called '*su jak* 수작' and is an expression of closeness like brothers. This practice has gradually disappeared although it regarded as an art because it is not only unhygienic, but also it encourages to drink immoderately. As the number of cars in South Korea is rising, drunken accidents are increasing greatly. So, Korean people do not press a drink on others.

Korean people drink alcohol not alone but together. This causes South Korea's alcoholic addiction rate to be relatively lower compared to other countries, although Korean people tend to drink too much. Generally, South Korean people change places and have a deep conversation during drinking. In the first round, they drink lightly with their supper and enter into the second and third rounds. Like a saying *chwi jung jin da*m 취중진담 (truth in wine), they speak from the heart when the number of rounds increases. They believe they become a true friend by drinking several times together in this way. It is connected to the patriarchy of South Korea. The two things lead men to go pub and talk their problems in work to male friends who are in the same condition. One is the idea that a husband and father should be always strong. The other is that fathers must shoulder on financial responsibility as shown in a saying 'I feed my family.' This psychological mechanism may be a natural process resulted from social pressure. Korean men drink themselves into a stupor and perform normal work in the next day. This can be called not only a tacit agreement in the Korean society but also a social drinking manner.

4. *Mak geol li* and *soju*

The representative Korean alcoholic beverage is *mak geol li* 막걸리 (rice wine).

It is called '*tak ju* 탁주' because it is muddy and milky. It is also called '*gok ju* 곡주' because it is mainly made from grain such as rice and wheat. It is made by fermenting a mixture of boiled rice and malted rice. It has relatively low alcohol content of six to seven percent so people drink it like a water when they are thirsty. Especially in hot summer days, a bowl of cold *mak geol li* after daily farm work helps quench their thirst instead of water and satisfy their hunger with this carbonated beverage - meaning, it is a health food as well as an alcoholic beverage. The glass for *mak geol li* is pretty bigger than other drinks. It does not need much eatables because the alcohol content of it is low. A piece of Korean pancake called jeon or kimchi is enough to prepare a liquor table. *Mak geol li* is a folk drink with folky flavor.

Other traditional liquors are ginseng liquor, *beop ju* 법주 in Gyeongju city and Andong *soju* 안동소주 in Andong city. South Korean people generally drink *so ju* 소주 and it is traditionally made by distilling grain and collecting the distilled dewdrops. The collected amount is very little. This is why Korean people made *so ju* containing chemicals. It is 'Chamisul' produced by HITEJINRO, Korean men's most favorite *so ju*, that belongs to those which contain chemicals. Beer and whisky were introduced to Korean by Western people after 1950's Korean War, but they are not as popular as *so ju*. The mass-produced *so ju* has low alcohol and is cheap. *So ju* was the typical liquor to forget the feelings of fatique from the 1960s to the 1970s,

Mak geol li

so ju

when all Korean people tightened their belt and worked hard. *So ju* is commonly imbibied alongside '*doe ji sam gyeop sal gu i* 돼지삼겹살구이 (Korean-style grilled pork belly)'.

Exercises

01 Read the following explanations. If they are right, put O in the
   brackets next to them. If they are wrong, put X instead.
   1) Given the Korean eating habit, Korean people have lower obesity rate
      than other counties. (   )
   2) *Guk*, one of Korean foods, can be drunken alone as same as soup. (   )
   3) The representative Korean traditional alcoholic beverage is *so ju*. (   )
   4) According to Korean table manner, people place the bowls of rice and
      soup on the table and do not hold them during a meal. (   )
   5) Kimchi is a fermented food and healthy food which prevents adult
      disease and cancer. (   )

02 Explain why Korean restaurants serve additional kimchi or soup
   for free.

03 Korean food is called slow food. Explain why and write the
   relevant Korean food.

04 List the traditional Korean drinking etiquette.

05 Choose your favorite Korean food and describe the characteristics
   of the food, the reason you like it and how to cook. And, talk to
   each other whether or not any food in your country is similar to
   Korean foods.

Chapter

6

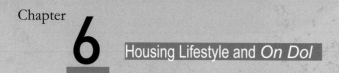 Housing Lifestyle and *On Dol*

You take off your shoes at home?

Step 1 Traditional *han ok*

1. Thatched-rood house and tile-roof house

Since old times, Korean people have emphasized the importance of the site of a house.

Korean people regarded as an ideal housing site a place where *yang* 양 (positive force) and *yin* 음 (negative force) are harmonized each other like *bae san im su* 배산임수 (a place where there is a mountain behind a house and where water flows in front of the house). Also Korean people prefer a house facing south which catches the sun and blocks out cold winds. Korean apartments which are usually spread out in a line reflect the preference of a southward house.

The traditional houses of Korea are called '*han ok*.' *Han ok* are divided into *cho ga jip* 초가집 (thatched-roof houses) and *gi wa jip* 기와집 (tile-roof houses). The name *cho ga jip* stems from the fact that the roofs are made by the spare straw left after harvesting. A wall covered with red clay emits an energy to prevent diseases. *On dol* installed underneath the floor keeps the house warm in winter and removes moisture in summer.

Gi wa jip have roofs which are made by weaving together roof tiles. They were usually lived in by *yang ban* 양반 (aristocrats). The point of a tiled roof has a natural curve which points up. The natural curving of *han*

Thatched house

Tile-roofed house

ok's roofs and *han bok*'s *jeo go ri* (traditional Korean jacket) is commonly chosen as examples of the beauty of Korea.

2. Structure of *han ok*

Han ok are briefly divided into two parts *ma ru* 마루 (covered wooden floor) and *gu deul* 구들 (Korean floor heating system) or *on dol*.

Because *ma ru* is open, it is cool in summer and warm in winter. *On dol* have developed in the cold northern part of Korea and *ma ru* in the southern part of it. The harmony of two different structures *ma ru* and *gu deul* is a special characteristic of *han ok* which is hard to find in other countries. It is very difficult to find the two structures in the Central China. Japanese houses have rooms with *ma ru* and *ta ta mi* たたみ (Japanese floor mat), they do not have a system of heating a stone floor by channeling heat from the kitchen furnace through under-floor flues, like *gu deul* or *on dol*.

Besides these structures, *han ok* are comprised of a low wall, a front gate, an open yard, *daet dol* 댓돌 (terrace stones), *ma ru*, room, *on dol*, a kitchen and *jang dok dae* 장독대 (a crockery terrace where the jars for soy sauce, bean paste, and red pepper paste are kept). *Han ok* are usually surrounded by a stone wall. When you go through the main gate of them, you can see tile-roof houses with an inner wing arranged in the shape of the letter 'ㄱ' or 'ㄷ.' The main building is made up by *an bang* 안방 (an inner room), *dae cheong* 대청 (covered wooden floors between rooms), *geon neon bang* 건넌방 (a room opposite the an bang), *sa rang bang* 사랑방 (men's room). Next to the main gate there are a barn, a storeroom and *haeng rang chae* 행랑채 (servants' quarters).

Korean walls were not high. The walls of normal people's thatched-roof houses were rather low, for they were comprised of earth and stones. It was not high enough to block out thieves or wild animals and it was just a

Arrangement of Korean-style house (floor, kitchen, wall and pot)

border between houses. The main gates of thatched-roof houses are made out of twigs. Because the interior is easily seen through the twig gates, the gates do not block other people going in. The walls of *han ok* are of a height that shows the interior. This reflects the trusting nature of Korean people. The walls of tile-roof houses are made by piling up stones and earth, and the main gate is made out of timber; so, it has a more closed interior than thatched-roof houses. Compared with other countries, *han ok*'s walls and main gates are relatively low and they have a open nature to strangers. Next to the main gate of a tile-roof house, there is *sa rang chae* 사랑채 (a detached house for men). If you go through the middle gates, you can find the place where only women live. This place is of a structure to divide men and women. In the back yard, there are a chimney through which smoke from a kitchen is emitted and *jang dok dae*.

Han ok have a structure where people walk through *ma ru* to the room. Before going onto *ma ru*, people take off their shoes and put them on *daet dol*. There is an old saying which says 'Thieves do not rob a house where shoes are arranged in order.' The saying basically means that people can see the attitude of the people in the house by seeing how their shoes are arranged. This shows that *han ok* are so open that people can see the shoes on the terrace stones. Because the southern part of the Korean peninsula is particularly warm, there are many houses with an inner wing arranged in the shape of the letter 'ㄱ' whose yards are very open.

The schools of Korea are similar to the houses. They have low walls and in front of the school gates, and you can clearly see the classes behind the wide playground. However, the walls and front gates of Chinese houses are so high that they cover the interior. In China the shape of schools are similar to that of houses. In most of China's schools, school buildings are right behind the school gate and the playground behind the buildings; hence, the interior of those buildings cannot not be seen.

Ma ru is made out of wood. There are *dae cheong ma ru* 대청마루 and *toet ma ru* 툇마루 (narrow wooden porch running along the outside of a room) connecting *an bang* and *geon neon bang*. *Dae cheong ma ru* was so wide that people could eat a meal, sleep and hold ancestral rites on it. It played the same roles as living rooms of today and was a place for the conversation between the family members.

The hostess usually lived in *an bang* connected to the kitchen. In the kitchen, there are *bu ttu mak* 부뚜막 (wood-burning stove) on which a rice kettle is *hung, a gung i* 아궁이 (kitchen furnace) to make a fire, and *sal gang* 살강 (kitchen shelf) where bowls are placed. Because meals were eaten in a room, people used to set the table in the kitchen and carry it to the room. There were a well and *jang dok dae* near the kitchen. Because basic seasonings were stored in *jang dok dae* all the year round, they were regarded very precious. These days refrigerators in apartments played a role such as *jang dok dae*, Korean people prefer bigger refrigerators.

In Seoul, there are Namsan Hanok Village and Bukchon Hanok Village near Anguk Station on Subway Line No. 3, where the traditional housing lifestyle can be felt. Particularly, you can see traditional Korean weddings admiring traditional Korean houses in Namsan Hanok Village.

Step 2 *On Dol* and Sedentary Lifestyle

Korean people take off their shoes at home.

Many foreigners wonder about this. In one word, it is because the floor is warm. Korean people have chairs in apartments and restaurants, but they prefer sitting on the floor. It is more so when it is cold. People can sit on the floor because it is warm. Since they sit on it frequently, there is no need for shoes. If people take off their shoes indoors, the place becomes that much cleaner.

In any country, people use a heater or a stove to heat their home. However, Korean people thought heaters are not enough to block the cold temperatures coming up from the ground. Koreans solved this problem by inventing *on dol* (warm stone).

On dol is a heating system which heats up the floor. It is operated by the mechanism of heat transmission. When firewood is burned in the kitchen furnace, the heat heats up *gu deul* (flat stones) under the floor, and thus the whole room become warmed up. The smoke from the kitchen furnace is emitted through the chimney. When a fire is made in the furnace, food can be cooked in the pot hung on the wood-burning stove. It is a highly thermal-efficient system which makes possible heating and cooking at the same time. The *on dol* floor is the heated *gu deul*. *On dol* warms up the floor for a long time. People can stay warm even in the cold winter. The *on*

Structure of *on dol*

dol floor is better for older people's health. The energy of *on dol* promotes blood circulation. However, it took a long time to heat up *gu deu*l. Further, it was difficult to heat up the whole floor evenly. The warmer part of an *on dol* floor is called *a raet mok* 아랫목 because it is placed closest to the kitchen furnace. *A raet mok* had many functions. It became a place for visitors or the elderly. After coming back home from an outing, people warmed up their frozen feet and hands under blankets spread on *a raet mok*. People wrapped up rice bowls in blankets and place them on *a raet mok*. *A raet mok* was a place where the history oral traditional history was done. Sitting on it, people enjoyed conversations and the elderly told stories to their grandchildren.

Also, a hot *a raet mok* was the place where women in childbed their bodies. hey spent months lying down on it. Their recovery was fast and they did not become sick after giving birth. This means that *on dol* has curing abilities. The *on dol* therapy using the heat from the heated red clay has the same effects as the present infrared-radiation efficacy. Children put their stomachs on the floor when they had stomach aches after eating something cold. This is because *on dol* had the efficacy.

On dol had made Korean people's unique lifestyle. Wherever they go, they do not leave out their electric pads to warm up the floor. It is known that a department store in America once sold a series of small electric blankets called 'Mini ONDOL.' This was a product of the prestigious company General Electric and it was advertised as a hit product.

Korean people are used to a sedentary lifestyle where they feel warm by putting they backs to the floor. The lifestyle has a wide range of uses for space application, and so not many kinds of furniture is needed. In foreign countries, a house is divided into bedrooms, dining rooms, and etc. Accordingly, a space is required for furniture such as dining tables. However, Korean rooms only need one table. When a table is set in *an bang* (an inner room), it becomes a place for eating and also becomes a place for study. When mattresses and blankets are spread out in the evening, it becomes a bedroom.

After eating dinner, the family members enjoyed their conversations sitting in a circle after spreading blankets on a hot *a raet mok* without the need of separating into their bed room. The bond between the members was naturally strengthened. So, the *on dol* floor in the sedentary lifestyle is a space which fits in with the characteristic of Korean family members treasuring one another.

Step 3 Apartments and Modern Architecture

By the spread of western culture, *han ok* became western-style houses.

As urbanization started to spread from the 1960s, instead of timbers briquetts were used to light the fireplace. When economic growth and city development started to quicken in the 1970s, apartments were rapidly built. Nowadays people can only see thatched-roof houses in the places designated as folklore village. Compared with the empty houses of the countryside, high apartment buildings in the city are being built by the day. Because recently apartment lifestyle became common, it is not too much to say that half the population of big cities lives in apartments. There is a rapid increase in people who live in apartments with steam heating rather than *on dol* and sleep in the bed other than on the floor.

However, Korean people still have the habit of 'keeping their back warm to sleep peacefully' whether a place to sleep is the bed or the floor. Thousands of years of customs enabled Korean people to develop a heating system similar to *on dol* for apartments. To circulate warm water, they install pipes for heating boilers under the floor. During the winter, the rest area called '*jjim jil bang* 찜질방 (Korean dry sauna)' is enjoyed by the older generations who want a hot floor. Because of the oil fluctuations and pollution, today the *on dol* heating of thatched-roof houses is being

Jamsil Sports Complex

brought to attention as an efficient energy conserving system. According to 'International Ondol Society', the *on dol* heating is 20% more efficient than the ventilator heating for stand-up lifestyle in energy.

Unlike houses for sedentary lifestyle, there are modern structures which boasts architectural beauty. For example, there are 63 Building, which is the highest building in the East, Jamsil Sports Complex, built for the Seoul Asian Games in 1986 and the Seoul Olympics in 1988, the Seoul World Cup Stadium, the Sejong Cultural Hall, the Seoul Arts Center and the Myeongdong Catholic Church, nicknamed a building which has a steeple. Particularly, the Myeongdong Catholic Church was completed in 1898 and it represents Catholicism in Korea. It is the only pure Gothic building in Korea.

Exercises

01 Read the following statements and if they are right, put O in the brackets, and if wrong put X instead.

1) Korean people prefer a house facing south which catches the sun. (   )

2) Korean walls are so high that the inside of houses cannot be seen at all. (   )

3) Korean people take of their shoes at home. (   )

4) Korean people prefer sitting on the floor than sitting on a chair. (   )

5) People can still see traditional thatched-roof houses in cities of Korea. (   )

02 Explain the traditional heating system of Korea.

03 Recently, what kind of housing form is common in Korean people who live in cities?

04 The sedentary lifestyle in Korea has an advantage that it has a wide range of uses for space application than the stand-up lifestyle in the West. Explain two or more examples of it.

05 Visit and look around Namsan Hanok Village in Seoul and other *han ok* villages. Because of the oil fluctuations and pollution, today the *on dol* heating of thatched-roof houses is being brought to attention as an efficient energy conserving system. Let's talk with each other about its advantages and disadvantages.

Korean History which Has Bounced Back up Like a Roly Poly through Loyalty and Filial Piety

1. Ancient Joseon period (2333 B.C.-108 B.C.)

In South Korea October 3 is a red-letter day on the calendar.

What is October 3? It is Foundation Day, the birthday of Korea. It marks the beginning of Korea and is one of the most celebrated national holidays in Korea. This is because the history of the Korean people began as Ancient Joseon, Korea's first kingdom, was established in 2333 B.C. So, the history of Korea is called 'a continuous history of 5,000 years' or 'a 5,000-year-old history.'

It is said that people have lived in the Korean Peninsula since several thousand years before the foundation of Ancient Joseon. Ancient Joseon was a theocracy state in the Bronze Age. In those days, most of people lived a sedentary lifestyle and did farming. Ancient Joseon's law had 'Eight Major Prohibitions', of which 3 ones are presently known. One of them is: 'a thief shall become a slave. If he repents his crime, he must pay the penalty of 500,000 jeon.' This shows that Ancient Joseon respected private property and was a well-ordered hierarchy society containing aristocrats and slaves. Ancient Joseon in its heyday had a wide territory over the northern part of the Korean Peninsula and the northeastern part of China. In the 1st century B.C., Ancient Joseon was under the threat of invasion from the

Han Dynasty, one of the neighboring countries, and came to the ground in 108 B.C.

Every country has its birth myth which enables people to share a history and a community spirit. The story related to Dangun's foundation of Ancient Joseon was recorded in 'sam guk yu sa 삼국유사(Memorabilia of the Three Kingdoms)' handed down to the present time.

The myth of Dangun, the founder of Ancient Joseon, is as follows:

Hwanin, the Emperor of Heaven had a son called Hwanung. The son yearned to live on the earth and to create a country which was benefit to people to realize humanitarianism. Hwanin let Hwanung fulfil his dream. Hwanung descended to Mount Taebaek, presumed to be Mount Baekdu today, with 3,000 helpers including his ministers of rain, clouds and wind and found sin si 신시 (City of God) to govern the world. One day, a bear and a tiger came to Hwanung and asked him to become human. Hwanung gave them 20 cloves and garlic and a bundle of mugwort, telling them to eat only this sacred food and remain out of the sunlight for 100 days. The tiger gave up, but the bearer was transformed into a beautiful woman. The bear-woman

Map of Ancient Joseon

Ungnyeo got married to Hwanung and gave birth to a son. It is her son that is Dangun.

Through the myth of Dangun, the inner side of Korean people can be looked into. That is to say, the myth reflects the thought of the god of heaven that the founder of a nation is the grandson of the god of heaven. This is related to the thought of respecting heaven and loving people for the betterment of the world in harmony between heaven and human beings. It has been said that Ancient Joseon was established based on the idea of humanitarianism to widely benefit people.

2. Three Kingdom Period (108 B.C.-676 A.D.)

Korean people are good at archery.

South Korea has won excellent results at archery in the Olympics. According to China's old records, Korean people were called dong i jok 동이족, which means 'people in the east who use big bows and arrows.' In the ancient history of Korea, Jumong, which literally means 'best archer', founded Goguryeo. The main character Jumong was described as the best archer in 'Jumong', the popular TV series telecasted years ago. Jumong and his son Onjo are historical figures of the Three Kingdom Period.

The Three Kingdom Period was composed of three kingdoms Goguryoe, Baekje and Silla.

The three kingdoms grew while repeating war and alliance to hold the Han River in their political and military aspects. Culturally, they embraced Buddhism and Chinese classics to advance academic disciplines and prosper Buddhism.

Goguryeo was established by Jumong in the northern part of the Korean

Peninsula near the Yalu River in 37 B.C. Its territory was greatly extended during the reigns of Gwanggaeto the Great and King Jangsu in the 5th century. It was expanded to the north into the territory of Ancient Joseon and to the south into the Han River basin. In Jilin Province of China there is the tombstone of Gwanggaeto the Great, which tells of the foundation of Goguryeo and the land that he conquered. Goguryeo's people had a firm and strong character because they improved their country in endless clashes with China. In particular, they were good horse riders and archers and

Map of Goguryeo during its golden age

endowed with a progressive spirit. We can know their enterprising spirit from Goguryeo's frescos, such as *ssang yeong chong* 쌍영총 (dual dragon tomb), which remain today. Because Korean people respect the spirit of Gwanggaeto the Great and Goguryeo's people, they visit its historical sites and make movies or TV serieses of it. For example, the TV series 'Tae wang sa sin gi (The Four Guardian Gods of the King)' is based on the legend of dragon and Gwanggaeto the Great, and Yong-Joon Bae plays the hero. You can enjoy the TV series feeling Korean

Korean TV drama 'Jumong'   Goguryeo tomb murals

Stele of Gwanggaeto the Greate of
Goguryeo

Korean TV drama 'The Four Guardian Gods of
the King'

people's spirit and culture in the ancient history.

Baekje was established by Onjo in the Mahan region in 18 B.C. and first located in the Han River basin. Today the region is divided into Ghungcheong-do and Jeolla-do. Because Baekje was located in the southwestern part of the Korean Peninsula, it played an important role in sea trade very early among China, Korea and Japan. Baekje exchanged cultures with China and conveyed the continental cultures, such as Buddhism and Chinese classics, to Japan.

Nakhwaam and Baekma

River keeping legend of the fall of Baekje

King Uija was the final ruler of Baekje. It has been said that leaving politics alone he was trapped in pleasure-seeking and had 3,000 court ladies. According to an legend, the 3,000 court ladies jumped to their deaths from a rocky cliff top overlooking a sheer drop to the Baekma River and the spot was named 'Nakhwaam', which literally means 'the rock of falling flowers', when Baekje was collapsed by an allied force of Silla and Dang. Nakhwaam is located in Buyeo, Chungchongnam-do.

There is a sad story about General Gyebaek, who was King Uija's loyal subject. In 660 Baekje was

Korean Movie 'Once Upon a Time in the Battlefield'

invaded by 50,000 Silla forces, supported by 144,000 Tang soldiers. General Gyebaek knew that Baekje could not win Silla because his country's luck ran out. He killed his wife and his children before going into the battlefield of Hwangsanbeol. General Gyebaek and his 5,000 troops fought against Silla, but were finally defeated.

The movie '*Hwang san beol* (Once Upon a Time in the Battlefild)' deals with the battlefield between Baekje's General Gyebaek and Silla's General Yu-Shin Kim in the history of unification of the three kingdoms done by Silla. In particular, the local color is well brought out by the use of dialects of Gyeongsang-do and Jeolla-do by characters in the movie.

Silla was established in the *Jinhan region* (now Gyeongsang-do) by in 57 B.C. Silla was founded by King Hyeokgeose Park, but it was ruled by three dynasties Park, Seok and Kim. A higher percentage of two family names Park and Kim in Korea is closely related to Silla's leading role in the history of Korea.

It is notable that there were three reigning queens Seondeok, Jindeok and Jinseong in Silla. Seondeok became its first reigning queen because of its *gol pum* 골품 (bone rank) system that only *seong gol* 성골 (sacred bone-ranked) people can become the king of Silla. The highest bone rank was *seong gol* and the second one was *jin gol* 진골 (true bone), consisting of people of royal blood on one side of the family and noble blood on the other. In 520 the bone rank system was formalized in the law under King Beopheung. In 632 the Kim dynasty did not have any sacred bone males available to take the throne, and so a sacred bone women became Queen Seondeok. There are many stories of Queen Seondeok that have been told to this day. For example, the following story shows that Queen Seondeok was a very wise ruller.

Queen Seondeok received a box of peony seeds from the Emperor Taizong of Tang accompanied by a painting of flowers of peony. Looking at the picture, she predicted that the flowers of those seeds would not smell. After that, the flowers bloomed from the seeds but they did not smell. So, her subjects asked her for the reason. She answered, 'If the flowers bloomed, there would be butterflies and bees around the flower in the paining.'

She spent her life as a bachelor and made Silla a culturally prosperous country.

Although Silla was the last of the three kingdoms to grow, it formed an alliance with Dang and overthrew Baekje and Goguryeo to unify the three kingdoms in the 7th century. It is *hwa rang do* 화랑도 (a strict code of conduct and highly disciplined training) that played a key role in unification. *Hwa rang* 화랑, literally means 'flowery youth', was an organization consisting of teenagers who took an oath of loyalty to their country and learned literary and martial arts. *Hwa rang* produced many generals, and General Yu-Shin Kim also came from this organization.

3. Periods of Unified Silla and Balhae (676-935)

There is a city through which a history of a thousand years flows.

The city is Gyeongju, called 'the museum without walls.' In Gyeongu there are many historic remains such as great royal tombs, Buddhist temples, pagodas, and royal palace sites. Among them, Seokguram grotto, Bulguksa temple, Gyeongju Historic Areas and Yangdong Folk Village were designated as World Heritage Sites by UNESCO. This is because Gyeongju was the capital of Silla and Unified Silla for a thousand years.

Silla unified the three kingdoms, but it did not occupy Goguryeo's former territory in western Manchuria. Although the unification was not complete, it has a historical significance because Unified Silla is the first country which motivated a homogeneous national culture to be created.

Seokgul Grotto

The political system of Unified Silla was an aristocracy. Silla had a great economic exchange with Tang, and so its foreign trade grew greatly. Bo-Go Jang was a powerful maritime figure who promoted sea trade. Jang built a sea kingdom through a triangle trade among Silla, Tang and Japan. The festival celebrating Bo-Go Jang, called 'King of the Sea', is annually held in Wando-gun, Jella-do. Also, there is the Jangbogo Memorial Center located in Shidao (石島), Shantung Province (山東省), China, visited by many people.

Unified Silla developed Buddhist arts and left many splendid cultural remains such as Bulguksa temple and Seokguram grotto, designated as World Heritage Sites by UNESCO. A Buddhist scripter entitled *mu gu geong gwang dae da ra ni gyeong* 무구정광 대다라니경 (Pure Light Dharani Sutra) was printed from wood blocks in the period of Unifed Silla and found in Sakyamuni Pagoda of Bulguk Temple. It is presumed that it was printed between 700 and 751. It is the world's oldest printed material. Although the wood blocks do not remain, it shows Unified Silla's printing technique.

In the late 8th century, Unified Silla started to decline as it was weakened by conflicts among the nobility intensified. Powerful local gentry groups appeared to rebel the central government and established Later Goguryeo and Later Baekje. The period of later three kingdoms continued for 30 years and the millennium kingdom United Silla finally ended in 935.

In 698 Balhae was founded by Jo-Yeong Dae, a former Goguryeo

General, in the northern part of the Korean Peninsula and Manchuria. Balhae had borders with the north of Unified Silla. Balhae was referred to as *hae dong seong guk* 해동성국 (the flourishing land in the East) in its golden age. In 926 Balhae was destroyed by Khitan. Many of Balhae's people moved into Goryeo after the fall of Balhae.

Map of Goreyo

4. Period of Goryeo (935-1392)

Where did the word 'Korea' come from?

In 918 Goryeo was founded by Geon Wang, who established Later Goguryeo. He named the kingdom 'Goryeo' to succeed to the spirit of Goguryeo's people. Goryeo's international trade was prevalent because it actively carried out the policy of interchange with its neighboring countries. Merchants from the faraway land of Arabia engaged in the trade. Goryeo was widely known as 'Corea' by the Arabian merchants in the world.

Goryeo succeeded to the tradition of Unified Silla's Buddhism and promoted Buddhism as the state religion. The print technology of Buddhist scriptures was developed while Buddhism was being propagated into the public. The metal typefaces were first invented in Goryeo, but the exact date of the

Goryeo celadon

Tripitaka Koreana

invention is difficult to identify. Gyu-Bo Lee (1168-1241) wrote in his book '*dong guk is sang guk jip* 동국이상국집 (Collected Works of Minister Lee of Goryeo)' that 28 copies of '*sang jeon gye mun* 상전계문 (Prescribed Ritual Texts)' were printed with metal characters. '*Jik ji sim gyeong* 직지심경 (Anthology of Great Buddhist Priests' Zen Teachings)', one of Goryeo's early metallographic works, was printed in 1377 and left as the world's oldest book printed with movable metal type. It was 78 years earlier than Germany's Gutenberg Bible published in 1455. Inlaid celadon porcelain, called 'Goryeo Celadon' is famous as the representative cultural heritage of Goryeo. The jade green color of it symbolizes long life and wealth in the East, and patterns were carved on the outside of it.

Goryeo started to be weakened by foreign invasions in the 13th century. Goryeo received 6 attacks from Yuan, which was founded by the Mongolian ruler Kublai Khan (1215-1294) to conquer the world. The Goryeo government moved its capital to Ganghwa Island to stand against the invasion of Yuan because it found that mounted nomads such as Mongolian people are bad at naval battels. All of Goryeo's people united against Mongolian troops during 40 years of war, but Goryeo finally signed a peace treaty with Yuan in 1270. During the war Goryeo's people engraved wood blocks with Buddhist scriptures while praying the Buddha for the safety in their country. Tripitaka Koreana was completed from 1236 to 1251. It is called Eighty Thousand Tripitaka because it was compiled with 81,137 blocks. Tripitaka Koreana has been preserved to this day at Hein Temple in Hapcheon, Gyeongsangnam-do, and it was evaluate as one of the most important and complete corpus of Buddhist texts in the world by the UNESCO committee. The depository of Tripitaka Koreana was designated as a UNESCO World Heritage Site.

In the late of Goryeo there was Mong-Ju Cheong (1337-1392) a highly respected scholar. He has been known as a representative loyal subject in the history of Korea. In those days Goryeo was weakened and confused by the relation with Yuan. The rising power led by Seong-Gye Lee asked Cheong to join a coup against the king to establish a new kingdom. Cheong remained faithful, and so he was murdered by five men on the Sonjuk Bridge after a banquet held for him by Bang-Won Lee, the fifth son of Seong-Gye Lee. Cheong is famous for his poem '*dan sim ga* 단심가 (Song of Single-Minded Devotion)' showing his royalty to Goryeo. The poem became a Korean literary masterpiece and he has been referred to as 'Symbol of Royal Subject.'

Though I die and die again a hundred times.

That my bones turn to dust, whether my soul remains or not.

Ever loyal to my Lord, how can this red heart ever fade away?

5. Period of Joseon (1392-1910)

Early Joseon Period

Seoul, the capital of Korea, has 600 years of history.

In Seoul there are many beautiful royal palaces amid high rise buildings. Seoul is an attractive city where the past and the present coexist. Deoksu Palace next to the City Hall Station has held a guard changing ceremony since 1996. The royal gate Daehan Gate is opened and closed at a given time. The gatekeepers with the costume of the Joseon period hold the ceremony.

In 1394 Seoul (then Hanyang) was designated as the capital city of Joseon by Seong-Gye Lee, who found Joseon in 1392. Confucianism was an anchor to establish the foundation of Joseon. Confucianism was an ethical and philosophical system developed from the teachings of the Chinese philosopher Confucius. Lee made Confucianism a religion to unite the people mentally. This is because he wanted to correct the side effects of Buddhism empowered in the periods of Silla and Goryeo. Joseon accepted a bureaucracy under Confucian percepts. Josoen was called a society ruled by *yang ban* 양반 (a group of scholar-landlord officials) because the system of public post was divided into *dong ban* 동반 and *seo ban* 서반. The word *yang ban* was origianlly used specifically for members of the two orders of officialdom: *dong ban* or *mun ban* 문반 (civil or literary officials) and *seo ban* or *mu ban* 무반 (military officials). The concept of *yang ban* existed in Goryeo and it was systemized and institutionalized in Joseon.

King Sejong the Great, Joseon's fourth king, expelled Jurchen tribes and established the present national boundary across the Yalu River and the Tumen River. In particular, King Sejong the Great has been called the greatest king in the history of Korea. He invented hangeul 한글 (a phonetic alphabet composed of eleven vowels and seventeen consonants) for the people. He also promoted scientific techniques. During his reign, sun dials and water clocks were produced and the world's first rainfall gauge was invented. These techniques greatly contributed to the development of agriculture of those days. So, the framework of Joseon's national system was completed and Joseon developed into a strong nation.

Map of Joseon

Jongno Street is a busy shopping district in Seoul. There was a big shop called *yuk uy jeon* 육의전 in the Joseon period. This shows that Joseon's systems and customs had a great influence on Korean people's lifestyle.

In the late 16th century, Joseon started to engage in party strife due to a split within the ruling classes. Because Joseon did not plan a proper measure against foreign countries, '*im jin woe ran* 임진왜란 (Japanese invasion of Korea)' was launched by Hideysohi Toyotomi in 1592. Joseon's military tried to defend against the enemy and were no match for Japanese troops armed with matchlocks. Seoul (then Hanyang) was occupied by the Japanese army 20 days after the outbreak of war. However, the seven year's struggle of Korean people enabled them to drive the enemy from the Korean Peninsula. Admiral Sun-Sin Lee, who are greatly admired as the greatest general, played a great role in defeating Japan. After the war, Joseon was invaded by Qing in 1636. The invasion is called '*byeong ja ho ran* 병자호란 (the Manchu War).'

The two invasions of the middle Josoen period triggered *sil hak* 실학 (pragmatic studies) asserting that politics and studies should be helpful to living. Each village had *seo dang* 서당 (schools to educate children Chinese classics) for people's general education as thoughts respecting the people appeared. The development of popular literature caused the creation of novels written in hangeul. The awakened consciousness of peasants created *pan so ri* 판소리 (a type of musical dram), *nong ak* 농악 (farmer's music) and *tal chum* 탈춤 (mask dance-drama).

As Joseon's representative cultural heritages, hangeul invented by King Sejong the Great and 'Turtle Ship' built by Admiral Sun-Sin Lee can be chosen. Paintings and calligraphy based on Confucianism flourished. Many royal palaces (e.g. Gyeongbok Palace, etc.) and castle gates (e.g. the Great South Gate, the gates of Suweon Hwaseong Fortress, etc.) were built. White porcelain and white slip ceramic ware were produced in the field of crafts. The two major types of ceramics show ordinary people's characteristics in those days.

Late Joseon Period and Japanese Colonial Period

The society of Joseon fell into great confusion from the 19th century. Joseon's class system started to be broken down through the purchase of *yang ban* status due to *se do* 세도 politics, which refers to an abnormal style of politics where power was manipulated by members of the queen's family. Peasant uprisings caused Joseon to consume its national power. On the other hand, externally, Western ships from several countries began to appear Joseon's coast to demand trade with it. Josoen adopted a policy of isolationism and did not open the door to foreign countries to protect the traditional order from the outside world. But, the neighboring country Japan prepared for invading Joseon as a steppingstone toward the extension of its power over the Chinese continent. Joseon's people spread their national movement against the preparation. In 1897 King Gojong changed his name to *kwang mu* 광무 (Martial Brilliance) and proclaimed the establishment of an independent '*dae han* 대한 (Great Korean) Empire.' However, he could not change the destiny of the perishing country.

Gwan-Soon Yu (on the top right end of the picture)
Commemorative photograph of officials of Provisional Government of the Republic of Korea

Joseon let the world know that Joseon is an independent nation. In 1910, 500 years of Joseon finally ended and was annexed by Japan.

Japan waged Sino-Japanese War (1894-1895) against Qing over control of Joseon and plundered Joseon's human and material resources. Korean people suffered great hardships by Japan's colonial rule after Japan plundered the sovereignty of Joseon in 1910. The Japanese government-general ordered all Korean people to change their original names to Japanese style names in 1939. The Japanese colonial government prohibited teaching hangeul at school in 1941. Nonetheless, Korean people continued the anti-Japanese movement in their suffering. In 1919 the spread of the March 1st Independence Movement across the Korean Peninsula astonished the whole world. The provisional government was established in Shanghai on April 11, 1919. Outside the Korean Peninsula, the provisional

Memorial Carving of March 1st Independence Movement

government carried out the independence movement and organized the Independence Army for armed resistance against Japan. Finally Korean people achieved liberation from 36 years of Japanese rule because of the end of World War II due to Japan's surrender.

When it comes to independence fighters during Japan's colonial period, Korean people cannot forget about the March 1st Independence Movement Day and Gwan-Sun Ryu. Korean people sing a song celebrating her 1 March every year. Ryu called people in a market place and handed out Korean flags. She urged them to take to the streets and participate in Korea's struggle for independence. Finally, Ryu was arrested by Japan's police. Shouting '*dae han dok rip man se* 대한 독립 만세 (Long live an independent Korea)!', she was beaten and tortured to death in a prison at the age of 18. She is called 'Korea's Joan of Arc.'

Song Celebrating Gwan-Sun Ryu

When I look up at the sky on March,

I come to think about Gwan-Sun Ryu.

Shouting the independence of Korea although she was imprisoned,

she breathed her breath missing the blue sky.

On March 1, 1919, 33 national representatives signed and read the Declaration of Independence at Pagoda Park in Seoul. They shouted *dae han dok rip man se* with students. The declaration is now recognized as the world's literary masterpiece. Korean students learn these beautiful sentences with their ancestors' spirit. Today the New Year is officially rung in by striking the bell 33 times at Bosingak, Jongno, Seoul. This ceremony is called *je ya eui jong* 제야의 종 (The New Year's Eve Bell). To admire the spirit of March 1st Independence Movement, the bell is stricken by 33 national representatives of the Korean people on March 1 every year.

Korean people suffered because of Japan's invasion. During this time period, they left many literary gems. This is because intellectuals wanted to inspire patriotism by expressing their grief over their lost nation in writing through portraying the inner world of people rather than by fighting with guns and swords against the Japanese government. There are many of their works where the grief is sublimated into beautiful sentences. Those works are important to Korean modern literature. Poems and novels of those days are in Korean textbooks. Many students love to recite them. Anyone of Korean people remember several works. Yong-Un Han's '*nim ui chim muk* 님의 침묵 (Your Silence)' and So-Wol Kim's '*jin dal lae* 진달래 (Azalea)' are representative poems.

6. Period of the Republic of Korea (1945-Present)

Korean history gave a big piece of homework to the Korean people of today.

Korean Movie 'Joint Security Area', which depicts the division of Korean into north and south

The unification of South and North Korea! That is the greatest desire and homework of Korean people. Korea is the only divided country in the world. In Korea there are words such as the country divided into South and North, Panmunjeom, and separated families. These words contain the tragedy of fratricidal war. As a result, every Korean young man has the duty to serve in the army. The two Korean films 'Joint Security Area (2000)' and 'Welcome to Dongmakgol (2005)' act as a reference for the modern history of Korea because they were set in Panmunjeom, which symbolizes the Korean War and the division of South and North Korea.

The division traces back to 1945. Korea has been a kingdom with a king as its head for thousands of years after the Ancient Joseon period. The system of kingdom was collapsed by Japan's occupation of Korea in 1910 and liberated from Japan in 1945. However, the time of liberation was followed by a turbulent time because there was not a new ruling system. Two political powers appeared which were respectively backed up by US and USSR in the Korean Peninsula. The Korean land was fated to be divided into South and North in 1948. In the South there was founded the Republic of Korea (or South Korea), a free and democratic country with a presidential system. On the other hand, in the North there was established the Democratic People's Republic of Korea (or North Korea), which joined the Communist Camp.

The Korean War occurred because North Korea suddenly attacked South Korea at dawn on the 25th of June, when the foundation of South Korea was not established. The UN helped South Korea by sending the UN multinational force from 16 countries. The war was suspended by the cease-fire agreement and the Korean land is still divided into South and North.

The modern and contemporary history of Korea shows a suffering time when Korean people were under Japanese occupation for 36 years and had a fratricidal war for 3 years. South Korea was in a desperate situation because the Seung-Man Lee administration (1948-1960) sat on a mountain of debt and the people had nothing to wear and eat. The administration was politically unstabled and President Lee attempted to prolong his rule through the election fraud. The protest against that was continued by students and citizens.

President Chung-Hee Park, a former general, started a new government in the early 1960s. Based on his powerful leadership, President Park solved the matter of survival of people who were ragged and starved and then he promoted South Korea's modernization through 'New Village Movement' and the education of national spirit. As a result, South Korea achieved such an amazing economic growth in barely 30 years that it made the so-called 'Miracle on the Han River' surprising the world. These days Korean people say, 'We have gotten to live better thanks to President Park.' Despite his contribution to Korean economic growth, in 1979 his administration ended because of side effects of his long-term seizure of power.

During the terms of Presidents Doo-Hwan Chun (1980-1988), Tae-Woo Roh (1988-1993), Young-Sam Kim (1993-1998), Dae-Jung Kim (1998-2003), Moo-Hyun Roh (2003-2008), Myung-Bak Lee (2008-2013), and Geun-Hey Park(2013-Present), South Korea achieved a continuous economic growth and finally became a country which ranked up and down the 10 top trading countries in the world. As an internet strong power, South Korea is keeping pace with globalization based on knowledge economy in the 21st century.

Step 2 People on Korean Currency

1. Hangul Creation and King Sejong the Great

The person in the portrait on the front of the 10,000-won note of Korean currency is King Sejong the Great.

King Sejong the Great (1397~1450) was the greatest king in the history of Korea. He was printed on the front of the 10,000-won bill, the highest value note of Korean currencies put in circulation until spring in 2009. King Sejong the Great left behind the most remarkable achievement hangul or *hun min geong eum* 훈민정음 (The Correct Sounds for the Instruction of the People) in the history of the world. Hangul is a scientific writing system which was ingeniously invented. The *hun min jeong eum* manuscript 훈민정음 해례본 on the writing system was registered as the UNESCO World Documentary Heritage in 1997. King Sejong the Great was a sage king who took care of the people like his own child. He created the Korean alphabet so that his people can have their own written language easy to learn. During his reign, the world's first rainfall gauge was invented to measure the amount of rain. He also promoted scientific techniques which greatly contributed to the development of agriculture of those days. This enriched people's lives. He was the greatest king who worked for his country and people in all fields such as publication, music, art and national defense.

King Sejong the Great was a benevolent king who by means of his virtue, ruled his subjects who was politically against him.

King Sejong the Great's official historygraphers were in the awkward situation because of the problem of whether or not to record Mong-Ju Cheoung and Jae Gil as loyal subjects history books. This is because the two people were highly respected scholars loyal to the Goryeo dynasty but rebellious subjects of the Joseon dynasty. The historygraphers were touched to tears when he said as follows:

King Sejong the Great

'Mong-Ju Cheoung and Jae Gil must be recorded as royal subjects. History always have winners and losers. The winners lead a history. But, if the winners turn all the losers into traitors, the history will cease to continue in the hands of them. If the Goryeo Kingdom's subject was royal to his dying dynasty, he was recorded as a royal subject in history books.'

10,000 won bill and Sejong the Great on the bill

The Korean drama 'Sejong the Great', broadcasted by KBS in 2008, can be used as a good reference to him. Also, the Royal Tomb of King Sejong in Yeoju, Gyeonggi-do has been a good study place to meet the greatest king in the history of Korea.

2. Joseon Period's great scholars I Lee and Hwang Lee

I Lee and Hwang Lee was engraved on the front of the 5,000-won bill and the 1,000-won bill of Korean currency, respectively. Both of them were the two most prominent neo-Confucian scholars in the Joseon period.

5,000 won bill and I Lee
on the bill

I Lee (1536-1584) is called 'Yul-Gok Lee.' It was said that Yul-Gok grew up in his mother's parents' house in Gangneung. Gangneung is a place which has boasted beautiful scenic mountains, sea and lakes since the old days. The place printed on the back of the 5,000-won note is his mother's parents' house Ojukheon in Gangneung, where he was born and lived with his mother Sa-Im-Dang Sin in his childhood.

The scholar Yul-Gok presented a revolutionary social policy to solve the problems of reality through study. In particular, he is famous for his proposal on training of 100 thousand soldiers. He argued that 100 thousand soldiers must be raised against a possible Japanese attack. His proposal was rejected by the government, but his prediction came true because of Japan's invasion to Joseon. In Paju, Gyeonggi-do, where he stayed, there are historical sites related to him, such as Hwaseok Pavillion and Jaun Seoweon, where he researched.

1,000 won bill and Hwang
Lee on the bill

Hwang Lee's (1501-1570) pen name is Toe-Gye. He was born in Dosan, Andong. His viewpoint of philosophy is that the truth exists in a normal life. In 1574 he established Dosan Seowon, an education institution which still exists in Andong. He was introduced into Japan after Japanese invasion of Korea in 1592. This had a great effect on Neo-Confucianism in Japan.

3. Turtle Ship and Admiral Sun-Sin Lee

100 won coin

The person in the portrait on the 100-won coin is Admiral Sun-Sin Lee (1545-1598).

When Japan invaded Korea in 1592, Admiral Sun-Sin Lee greatly defeated the Japanese navy at sea using *geo buk seon* 거북선 (Turtle Ship) and protected his country from the enemies. Turtle Ship is the world's first ironclad battleship built in the late 16th century.

In particular, Turtle Ships built by Admiral Lee destroyed 122 Japanese battleships. This made the best record in the world history of naval battels. You can feel Admiral Lee's historical footprints in Hansan Island, which lies in the coastal waters of Tongyeong-si, Gyeongsangnam-do. Because he was good at writing, he left behind many works of literature such as 'A War Diary.' Among those works, there is the following poem 'Hansan Island', which made people sad about the fact that the beautiful sea would be the battlefield.

General Sun-Sin Lee

All alone, I see the moon so bright, as I sit on

fortress walls.

My sword held close tonight I keep the watch with anxious heart.

Yet somewhere in the darkened night, a pipe lulls worry away.

The common thing about Korean currency put in circulation at the present time is that the people in the portraits on the notes and the coin of them are people in the period of Joseon, that is, highly literate king or scholars. This means that Korean people are proud of the fact that Korea was not ruled by the military, its culturally advanced intellectuals protected their history and they gave its tradition to the neighboring countries as civilized people of '*dong bang ye ui ji guk* 동방예의지국 (the country of courteous people in the East)', although it was a small country adjacent to a large country.

By the way, the people in the portraits on the notes of Chinese currency are contemporary politicians such as Ze-Dong Mao 毛 澤東(1893-1976) and En-Lai Zhou 周恩来 (1898-1976). Japan printed cultured people in modern times such as So-Seki Natsu-Me 夏目 漱石 (1867-1916) on the notes of Japanese currency and South Korea classical scholars in the Joseon period.

4. Korea's representative woman Sa-Im-Dang Sin

A 50,000-won note was issued newly in spring in 2009.

The person in the portrait on the note is Korea's representative woman Sa-Im-Dang Sin. The fact that a woman was accepted as a portrait on the note for the first time in South Korea can be a mirror of the time which calls people's attention to the importance of education and home.

50,000 won bill and sin sa im dang on the bill

Sa-Im-Dang Sin was a woman in the middle Joseon period who was an example of good wife and wise mother. She excellently fulfilled the duties of a woman to her husband and children and left many works by developing her abilities and talents. Because she was excellent in poetry, prose and fine arts, she has been called the best woman painter in Korea. Above all things, she raised her son into such a wise person that she has been praised as the mother of the great neo-Confucian scholar I Lee.

Exercises

01 Read the following statements. If they are true put O in the (　),
and if not put X instead.
1) The English name of Korea comes from the word 'Corea' in the
Goryeo period. (　)
2) Seoul is the oldest city in Korea which has '1,000 years of
history.' (　)
3) Sa-Im-Dang Sin is the person in the portrait on the front of the
50,000-won note of Korean currency which was issued newly. (　)
4) Korean people respect the spirit of Goguryeo's people who expanded
their territory greatly. (　)
5) Turtle Ship is an ironclad battleship built by Admiral Sun-Sin Lee in
the period of Joseon. (　)

02 Who is the person in the portrait on the front of the 10,000-won
bill of Korean currency? Write all the achievements of him you
know about.

03 Korean people have had the greatest desire and homework since
June 25, 1950. What is that?

04 South Korea has won excellent results at archery in the Olympics.
Let's find traces of Korean people's superiority in archery in
Korean history and talk about them.

05 The story related to Dangun's foundation of Ancient Joseon was handed down to the present time. Write all you know about this myth. Also, let's talk about the birth myths of your country.

Do you know the division of South and North Korea and 'Miracle on the Han River'?

Step 1 Democracy and the Division of South and North Korea

1. President and administration

Presidential system

According to the Constitution of the Republic of Korea, the president represents the country and is the chief executive of the government, commander-in-chief of the armed forces, and the head of the state of the Republic of Korea. The president is directly voted by the citizens and limited to a single 5-year term. As the supreme ruler of the country, the president represents the country when dealing with foreign affairs. He or she has general authorities to declare treaties, a diplomatic delegation, war and a state of national emergency, to arbitrate in a dispute among three branches of government the legislative, the executive and the judicial, to demand to summon an extraordinary session of the National Assembly and to nominate constitutional judges, the Chief Justice of the Supreme Court and the prime minister.

Korea's presidential system began on the 17th of June, 1948 (Constitution Day) when the constitution was promulgated. Here is a list of the presidents of South Korea: Seung-Man Lee (1st, 2nd & 3rd terms, 1948-1960), Bo-Seon Yun (4th term, 1960-1962), Chung-Hee Park (5th, 6th, 7th, 8th & 9th terms, 1963-1979), Gyu-Hah Choi (10th term, 1079-

1980), Doo-Hwan Chun (11th & 12th terms, 1980-1988), Tae-Woo Roh (13th term, 1988-1993), Young-Sam Kim (14th term, 1993-1998), Dae-Jung Kim (15th term, 1998-2003), Moo-Hyun Roh (16th term, 2003-2008), and Myung-Bak Lee (17th term, 2008-2013), and Geun-Hye Park (18th term, 2013-present).

It is said that Korean people are relatively interested in politics. They had many names for their leader and government. Generally the period ruled by President Seung-Man Lee is called 'Liberal Party Era', President Chung-Hee Park the era of the 'Third and Fourth Republic' and Doo-Hwan Chun the era of 'Fifth Republic.' The administration of presidents has been called 'Civilian Government' since Young-Sam Kim, who was not the military leader, was inaugurated in 1993. Nowadays, the word *jeong bu* 정부 (government)' is mainly used to refer to the administration, as shown in *guk min jeong bu* 국민정부 (the government of people) and *cham yeo jeong bu* 참여정부 (participatory government).

Seung-Man Lee, the first president of South Korea, constructed the foundations of democratic republic, but he experienced the years of poverty and hardships caused by political division and the tragic, destructive fratricidal war Korean War.

President Park Geun-hye
President Jeong-Hee Park and
New Village Movement

President Chung-Hee Park led a military coup on May 16, 1961 and tided over South Korea's chaotic state of affairs in South Korea based on the military spirit. In the beginning of the 1960s, President Park made a 5-year economic development plan to escape the fact that South Korea was the world's poorest country in those days, under the slogan 'Let's live better.' He issued 'The Charter of National Education' to put hope in the people who suffered from the pain of the Korean War and enlighten their spirit. He made foundations for South Korea's economy. He started New Village Movement, which led to better life in the urban areas, and achieved South Korea's economic revival called 'Miracle on the Han River.' He is acknowledged as a leader who made Korean people to be industrious and have an enterprising spirit under the slogan 'We can do it' to develop South Korea into a great economic power in the world. Despite his achievements, his long-term seizure of power brought him into conflict with the people.

The Doo-Hwan Chun administration had great conflicts with the people because of Gwangju Democratization Movement, which occurred on May

Intra-Korean Summit

18, 1980 before Chun's first presidential inauguration on September 1, 1980. However, President Chun achieved a continuous economic growth in South Korea during his second presidency. The achievement motivated the Tae-Woo Roh administration to hold the 1988 Seoul Olympics.

The Young-Sam Kim administration was called 'Civilian Government' in the sense that Kim's presidential inauguration in 1993 put the line of military rule to an end.

President Dae-Jung Kim was a person who had acted as a leader of opposition part for a long time. He took special interests in the division of South and North Korea and issued 'Sunshine Policy' against North Korea. President Dae-Jung Kim was the first president of South Korea who visited North Korea to have an inter-Korean summit during the presidency. In 2000 President Dae-Jung Kim was awarded the Nobel Peace Prize for his contribution to bring about a reconciliation between South and North Korea and to lessen the tension of East Asia for world peace.

Geun-Hye Park was inaugurated as the 18th president of South Korea in 2013 and South Korea's first female president. As a leader who had a long political career for a long time by the influence of her father President Jung-Hee Park, she is putting as objectives of her adminstration the fulfillment of the happiness of the people and the welfare of South Korea.

Executive branch

The executive branch is commonly called government and an organization which manages the administrative affairs of the country. The government organization is made up of the State Council headed by the president and administrative agencies.

The presidential residence 'Blue House' is part of the executive branch. The executive branch consists of 2 offices the executive office of the president and the executive office of the prime minister, 2 agencies

Ministry of Government Ministry and Ministry of Patriots & Veterans Affairs, 3 commissions Anti-Corruption & Civil Rights Commission of Korea, Financial Services Commission and Fair Trade Commission, 17 ministries Ministry of Strategy and Finance, Ministry of Education, Ministry of Foreign Affairs, Ministry of Unification, Ministry of Justice, Ministry of National Defense, Ministry of Security and Public Administration, Ministry of Culture, Sports and Tourism, Ministry of Agriculture, Food and Rural Affairs, Ministry of Health & Welfare, Ministry of Environment, Ministry of Employment and Labor, Ministry of Gender Equality & Family, Ministry of Land, Infrastructure and Transport, Ministry of Oceans and Fisheries, and Ministry of Science, ICT and Future Planning, and 15 administrations (e.g. National Tax Service, Korea Customs Service, Korea Meteorological Administration). Besides these, there are government-affiliated public organizations such as Korea Tourism Organization.

The government's flag is raised in front of the building of a public organization. The people who work in the organization are called public officials. Public Officials are ranked as Grades 1 to 9 and Grade 9 is the lowest one.

South Korea is enforcing a local self-governing system. The self-governing units consist of higher-level (provincial) governments (e.g. metropolitan city and province) and lower-level (municipal) governments (e.g. si, gun, gu and myeon). Currently, there are 16 higher-level governments: Seoul, the capital city of South Korea, 6 metropolitan cities (e.g. Busan, Daegu, Incheon, Gwangju, Deajeon and Ulsan) and 9 provinces (e.g. Gyeonggi-do, Chungcheongnam-do, Chungcheongbuk-do, Jeollanam-do, Jeollabuk-do, Gyeongsangnam-do, Gyeongsangbuk-do, Gangwon-do and Jeju-do). Each city including Seoul has its mayor and city council. Every province has its governor responsible for all affairs of the provincial administration and members of the provincial assembly. Governors, mayors, members of city council and members of provincial assembly are directly elected by the people.

There are three types of elections held in South Korea: (1) presidential election, (2) national assembly election and (3) local government election (to choose a mayor, a governor and the head of gu).

2. National assembly and legislation

The National Assembly is South Korea's representative organization which exercises the legislative power to reflect the will of the people. It is South Korea's highest decision-making body which as the legislative branch enacts laws, deliberate budgets and decide important policies.

The members of the National Assembly has a 4-year term. Two-thirds of the members are elected by popular vote. The remaining seats are distributed proportionately among parties winning five seats or more in the direct election. The total number of Assembly members provided by the Constitution is no less than 200.

The National Assembly has 1 speaker and 2 vice-speakers. The speaker and the vice-speakers are elected by a majority vote of the incumbent Assembly members and have a 2-year term. There are two sessions of the Assembly: regular and extraordinary. The ordinary session opens September 1 every year and its duration is no more than 100 days. The extraordinary session is held by the request of the president or a quarter or more of the Assembly members, and its duration is no more than 30 days.

Let us think of South Korea's party politics. There are political parties in the National Assembly. South Korea has a multiparty system and there have been many political parties in South Korea since the establishment of the Republic of Korea in 1948. Generally, the political parties are divided into the ruling party and the opposition parties. South Korea a presidential system, and hence the president is from the ruling party. Here is the list of the ruling parties in South Korea: Liberal Party led by President Seung-Man Lee, (Democratic) Republican Party led by President Chung-Hee Park, (Democratic) Justice Party, (Democratic) Liberal Party, Grand National Party, Democratic Party, Our Open Party and New Frontier Party.

The National Assembly of South Korea meets in the National Assembly Building located in Yeouido. It is the building's green roof in the background of the beautiful Han River that you can see even from afar. You can see people stage a protest against what they feel inconvenient in front of the National Assembly Building. This can be seen as a natural part of a democratic society. People can visit the assembly building except when the regular session is held or on a special day. However, they must make an on-line reservation at the its website for a visit to the assembly.

3. Judiciary and media

Judiciary

South Korea is a constitutional state. The constitution is the system of fundamental laws and principles that prescribes the nature, functions, and limits of a government and another institution. All other laws are subordinate to the constitution. The Korean Constitution was established and announced on July 17, 1948. The day called 'Constitution Day' was designated as a public holiday to celebrate the establishment. Article 1 of Korean Constitution consists of the following two clauses:

1. The Republic of Korea is a democratic republic.
2. The sovereignty of the Republic of Korea belongs to the people, and all authority comes from them.

As specified in the constitution, the people are the owner of the country. The country is run by the politicians and the people based on the constitution. Amendments to the constitution shall be proposed by the agreement of two thirds or more of the Assembly members and passed by a referendum. The constitution states the basic rights and duties of the people. The people have the freedom of residence, occupation, religion, assembly and association and a suffrage. On the other hand, they have duties of national defense, tax, education, work and environment conversation.

In South Korea, there is a special organization called the Constitutional Court. The Constitutional Court is a special court designed to rule on whether or not laws that are in fact unconstitutional, that is whether or not they conflict with constitutionally established right and freedoms. This means that the constitution must be enforced more strictly because it is fundamental to all laws. As an independent organization, the constitutional court is made up of 9 judges who cannot join a political part and intervene in politics to make a fair and impartial judgement. Chief Justice of the Constitutional Court is appointed by the president.

In South Korea the Supreme Court is the highest court in South Korea. The Chief Justice of the Supreme Court is the head of the judical branch of South Korea and has a single 6-year term. He or she is appointed by the president with the consent of the National Assembly. There are three tiers of courts in South Korea: the District Courts, the High Courts and the Supreme Court. The District Courts are the courts of original jurisdiction, the High Courts the intermediate appellate courts, and the Supreme Court the highest court. South Korea adopted a three-tiered judicial system which allows the erroneous rulings of lower courts to be corrected by higher tribunals in three tiers.

People must pass the bar examination to be a judge, a prosecutor or a lawyer.

Media

Korea is country which grants the freedom of speech. The media is made up of television stations, radio stations, cable stations, news agencies, newspapers, and publishers. There are three main TV networks called terrestrial broadcasting stations: Korea Broadcasting System (KBS), the Munwha Broadcasting Company (MBC) and Seoul Broadcasting System (SBS). KBS is the state-controlled network and divided into KBS-1 and KBS-2. KBS-1 is supported indirectly by viewers via subscription fees, but KBS-2 is supported through advertisement. Further, there are Educational Broadcasting System (EBS) and Arirang TV. In particular, Arirang TV delivers programs worldwide via satellite for 24 hours a day to overseas Koreans and Korean people who reside abroad.

The age of satellite broadcasting has come to Korea since the satellite Mugunghwa was launched in 1995. Skylife is the representative satellite broadcaster. Besides this, there are cable TV networks. Cable TV programs are lack of public interest, but they can supply information of vast areas, such as movie, music, drama, religion, home shopping, etc. When it comes to radio broadcasting, many of broadcasting companies provide AM and FM radio services. For example, there are religious broadcasting stations, such as Christian Broadcasting Station (CBS, Protestant), Far East Broadcasting Corporation (FEBC, Protestant), Pyeonghwa Broadcasting Corporation (PBC, Catholic) and Buddhism Broadcasting System (BBS, Buddhist), in addition to Seoul Traffic Broadcasting System (TBS) and music radio stations. In the future, many types of media environments such as internet and digital broadcasting will be accessible due to the faster development of IT technology.

The 5 representative newspapers of Korea are Dong-A Ilbo (1920),

Representative Korean daily newspapers

Chosun Ilbo (1920), Hankook Ilbo (1954), Joong-Ang Ilbo (1965), and Hankyoreh (1988). As being established in the 1920s, Dong-A Ilbo and Chosun Ilbo have relatively many older generations of readers. There are local newspapers (e.g. Daegu Maeil, Kwangju Ilbo, etc.) and religious newspapers, such as Bulgyo Sinmun (Buddhism) and Kukmin Ilbo (Protestant). Because recently newspaper companies are operating an online newspaper system, readers can easily access any media source.

Also, there are many online bookstores such as YES 24 (http : // www.yes24.com). People can search and order book(s), and request the international shipping of them, on the internet.

In South Korea, there is Korea Press Foundation (http : // www.kinds.or.kr), which helps the press express its views freely. Sometimes the press can damage people because of their distorted reports. To help the problem, the government established Press Arbitration Commission, which supplies counselling services for victims of the press and helps them get relief from the damage.

4. Division of South and North Korea and foreign policy

Ceasefire line and panmunjeom

The ceasefire line is the division line between South and North Korea.

The Korean War is the event when a war between South and North Korea that took place on the 25th of June, 1950. It is a historical fact that hurts the hearts of many korean people today.

Korean people have longed for the reunification of Korea. Now they perceive it as their obligation. The historical background of the Korean War goes back to the days when Korea was liberated from Japan on the 15th of August, 1945. Korean people were only able to gain liberty from Japan by the countless numbers of liberation movements and the victory of the Allied Forces in World War II.

After World War II, Korean people wanted an independent nation with a new ruling system. In those days, the Free World led by US and the Communist camp led by USSR were under conflicts.

Two political powers appeared which support respectively US and USSR in the Korean Peninsula. the Korean land was divided into two parts South and North, with the 38th parallel line. On the 15th of August, 1948, the Republic of Korea was founded in the South and the Democratic People's Republic of Korea in the North. So, Korea is still divided into South and North Korea.

North Korea, supported by the Soviets, suddenly attacked South Korea at dawn on the 25th of June, 1950. Seoul was captured by North Korea just 3 days later after the outbreak of the Korean War and the other areas 1 month. The UN helped South Korea by sending the UN multinational force from 16 countries. General McArthur, the then supreme commander of the UN force, succeeded in Incheon Landing Operation and advanced to the Yalu River. Because of China's intervention, hard battles continued.

Panmunjeom (the discussion area between South and North Korea in the demilitarized zone)

At last, the cease-fire agreement of the Korean War was signed by North Korean, Chinese and the UN forces but the South Korean refused to sign. It is the ceasefire line that is the military demarcation line (DML) decided by the agreement.

The Demilitarized Zone (DMZ) is a buffer zone between South and North Korea which runs along the ceasefire line and is 250 kilometers long and 4 kilometers wide. Panmunjeom is in the DMZ and it is the place where the cease-fire agreement of the Korean War was signed. The Joint Security Space of Panmeunjeom has a 800-meter distance between the UN and North Korean forces. This place is open to foreign tourists except people from some countries.

The movie 'Joint Security Area (2000)', set in Panmeunjeom, shows well the sad reality of the division of South and North Korea. Because of the reality, South Korea adopted a conscription of all men. In other words, Korean young men have the duty to go to the army after receiving a physical examination when they are 18 years old.

South Korea's diplomatic policy

South Korea has diplomatic relationships with most countries. According to the 2005's statistics, South Korea had diplomatic relationships with 185 countries and it had 130 diplomatic establishments: 95 resident embassies, 31 consulate generals and 4 representatives.

Through active diplomatic activities, South Korea has developed friendly relations with US, China, Japan and Russia. The Korean-American relation is the most friendly one. The Korean-Japan relation was set up through the 1965's diplomatic normalization between South Korea and Japan. South Korea has tried to drive away negative feelings against Japan's forcible occupation of Korea and to strengthen security and economic cooperations with Japan. There was a severance of diplomatic relations between South Korea and China because of differences in their ideology although historically they maintained friendly relations with each other. But, South Korea established diplomatic ties with China in 1992. Recently China is becoming a country visited most frequently by Korean people for study and business. In addition to friendly relations, South Korea has continued to push an active polity for the unification of Korea.

South Korea joined the UN in 1991 and many international

Korea's joining in international organizations

| IMF (1955) | APEC (1989) | United Nations (1991) | WTO (1995) | OECD (1996) |

Ki-Moon Ban, the 8th United Nations Secretary-General

organizations to take an active part in the international arena. Ki-Moon Ban is a Korean who is the eighth and current Secretary-General of the United Nations. He is a proud Korean who since 2007 has been received as a head of state and tried to achieve the peace and common prosperity in the world while cooperating with the world's political leaders. Ban was reelected by the representatives of member states of the UN on 21 June, 2011 and will continue to serve until December 31, 2016.

Step 2 New Village Movement and Miracle on the Han River

1. The characteristics of the economic development of South Korea

South Korea was a traditional farming country even until 50 years ago. Korean people were not able to even try to achieve industrial modernization in the beginning of the 20th century because of Japan's forcible exploitation of Korea during the late Joseon period and Japan's colonial era and of the Korean War. Only old war wounds and poverty were left behind.

However, the South Korean government started the first 5-year economic development (1961-1966) and completed the sixth 5-year economic development (1982-1986). The six developments achieved an average of high economic growth rate (8.6%). South Korea underwent a fast economic growth called 'Miracle of the Han River.' Because of this, Korean people's willingness and industriousness were recognized by the world. The causes and characteristics of South Korea's economic growth are as follows.

The first one is a government-led export policy.

The characteristic of South Korea's economic growth is 'Super-high

Growth.' This is because the export-driven policy was led by the government. Because South Korea lacked in material resources but had many human resources, it carried out the strategy of processing trade through the introduction of foreign capital and the import of raw materials. As a result, South Korea a rapid economic growth

The first ceremony of Day of Export (1964)

rate (9.9%) during 1960 and 1978. During this period, South Korea's growth national product (GNP) per capita increased from 60 dollars to 3000 dollars and the then agriculture country South Korea changed to an industrial nation. In those days, the poorest nation's GNP per capita was 60 dollars. South Korea fulfilled the 10 billion dollar goal for exports in 1977. Exports continued to play a bigger role in South Korea's economic growth after that time. The percentage of South Korea's reliance on export was 65% in the 2000s. The Guro area in Seoul was created as an export industrial complex called 'Guro Export Industrial Complex', and it represented industrialized areas in South Korea. The area has been called 'Guro Digital Complex' since high-tech industries such as IT played a great role in South Korea's economy in the 2000s.

The second one is the success of New Village Movement.

New Village Movement can be the driving source behind what led the success of South Korea's industry modernization in the 1970s. President Chung-Hee Park started the nation wide campaign called 'New Village Movement' to modernize rural areas and created a strong emotional impetus for South Korea's development. He wrote and composed the song of New Village Movement to free the people from poverty and let them have diligence.

The daybreak bell has rung, it is now a new day
Let's all get up and make a new village
Let's make our new village ourselves

In addition to this song, there was a song called 'Let's live well.' In those days, these songs could be heard all over the country. Everyone who heard these songs worked hard. People in rural areas recreated their village to a more livable one. They replaced their thatch-roof houses to new ones, used tap water instead of the well and used electricity instead of candles. Young people were trained as community leaders of their areas. University students in cities participated in volunteer work at rural areas. In every school, 'The Charter of National Education' was read aloud during the morning meeting every day to give students a sense of pride in their country. The government actively developed the mass-education campaign that the people should work harder and make their country better to live a blameless life for their ancestors and descendants.

The final ones are excellent human resources and Confucian values.

Plenty of excellent human resources based on education were the greatest factor of South Korea's economic growth. Since the old days, Korean people have had the values that people should learn to survive even if they were poor. Under the values, they worked harder day and night with the hope of living better. Korean people have had a diligent heart which cannot be seen in any other country.

It can be said that Confucian human relations also played an important role in South Korea's economic growth. In other words, Korean people regarded their workplace as their homes. The CEO takes care of the company's workers as if they were his or her children. The workers stay after the closing time to achieve the goals of the company. Because of the strong endurance, sacrifice, and cooperation of these excellent human resources, there was nothing that Korean companies could not do although those things that foreigners thought impossible.

2. Story of the foundation of Korean economy

In the 1960s out of the 120 nations in the UN, South Korea was the second poorest country. The foreign press regarded South Korea as a country which could not be reborn and took no interest in it. In this situation how did South Korea raise funds to achieve its economic growth?

It may be commonly believed that South Korea received those funds from US and other Western countries. Of course, there was much aid from those countries. However, the hard situation could be overcome by the endurance of President Chung-Hee Park and the people's will of a better life. The following is the behind story of the introduction of foreign capital which was a good stepping stone to South Korea's economic growth which was published as the title 'Tears of the President' in the magazine 'Rotary Korea.'

After the success of a military coup on May 16, 1961, General Chung-Hee Park requested US economic aid for South Korea's economic reconstruction, the President of US Kennedy did not recognize the revolutionary government. General Chung-Hee Park crossed the Pacific Ocean and went to the White House to meet President Kennedy, but his request was denied. After returning to the hotel, General Park and his entourage kept shedding tears without end while packing their luggages because they would come back empty-handed to their country. There was not any country that would borrow money to the poor country. As a last resort, President Park thought of West Germany. In those days, West Germany was the same situation as South Korea because Germany had been divided into West and East Germany after World War II. At last, he succeeded in borrowing 140 million mark from West Germany. In return, South Korea agreed to send nurses and miners to West Germany and impignorate their wages.

There were 46 thousand applicants for the job of 500 mine workers with a high school diploma who would be sent to West Germany. Many of the applicants were university graduates. They rubbed their hands with black briquettes to make them rough look like a laborer's rough hands in case they would fail a job interview because of their smooth hands. 123 mine workers were sent to West Germany in 1963.

The nurses who had arrived in West Germany were scattered to different hospitals in rural areas. The first duty of the nurses is to clean the deceased because they had difficulties in communicating in German. In the geothermal heat, the miners worked hard in underground mines located more than 1,000 meters below ground. Compared with Western German people who only worked 8 hours a day, these Korean workers mined coal for more than 10 hours in underground mines. West Germany's broadcasting networks and newspapers praised Korean female nurses and male miners, calling them a spectacular race. They said, 'How could anyone in the world do such hard jobs?' and called them 'Korean Angles.'

A few years later, President Chung-Hee Park visited West Germany by the invitation of Western Germany's President Heinrich Lübke. President Park's company went to an underground mine with President Lübke to encourage Korean mine workers. When President Park entered the hall, the faces of the miners wearing working clothes were streaked with black. Because they were choked with tears, President Park and the mine workers could not do it properly when they sang the Korean national anthem in unison before his speech. Then, President Park made his speech. He was lost for words as he looked at the miners who had come to this strange land and worked so hard in the underground mine more than 1,000 meters below ground that their faces were streaked black just because their country was poor. In a voice choking up with tears, President Park only repeated the sentence 'Let's work harder for our descendants.' In a foreign land far away from home, the male miners went through hardships underground several thousand meters and the female nurses worked harder at the hospital while cleaning the body of foreigners, just because they were citizens of a poor country. President Park could not hold back the tears any longer when thinking of the people who were starving back in his country. The miners bowed in front of President Lübke and said between sobs, 'Thank you, please help South Korea. Please help our president.' They countlessly repeated the sentence 'We will do our best whatever we do.' Even President Lübke was crying.

President Park kept crying in the car while returning to the hotel. Then he clenched his fists. When President Park was making a speech in front of the National Assembly of West Germany, he repeated the sentence 'Please lend South Korea some money. South Korea shall repay you. South Korean citizens never lie.'

The people of the country without any natural resources cut their hair and made wigs to sold them abroad. The elderly in rural areas cut their hair to support the educational fee of their sons and to buy rice. That is how Korea's wig industry developed. The campaign 'Rat Catching Movement' was started to export the product 'Korean Mink' made of rat hair. Everything that was of monetary value was sold. South Korea fulfilled the one hundred million dollar goal for exports in 1964. The world was surprised. The world looked with marveling eyes and wondered how a poor country can export one hundred million dollars worth of goods.

South Korea's companies joined construction projects of Middle Eastern countries in the 1970s. In these countries, South Korean workers made the impression that the only citizens that would work without rest in the hot desert were Korean people. In order to contribute to South Korea's modernization, those workers earned money while getting hit by sand storms and shedding a lot of sweat and tears. So, Korean people promoted national power enough to hold the 1988 Seoul Olympics and the 2002 FIFA World Cup.

Step 3 Today's Korean Economy

South Korea was one of the poorest farming countries in 1960. After that time, South Korea achieved an astonishing economical development for 30 years to be a newly industrialized country. Because South Korea grew enough to hold the 1988 Seoul Olympics, it became a role model for other countries. However, in 1997 South Korea started to experience a foreign exchange crisis because of the side affects of fast growth and political and economic factors together with the overall decline of the economy of Asia. The bailout incident of IMF gave a great shock and an economical confusion to the Korean citizens.

However, Korean people overcame the hardship by 'Gold Collection Campaign.' They overcame the national bankruptcy state only in 2 years, by donating their precious things, such as gold necklaces and gold rings, to the government. So, they made their country to be the fifth largest foreign exchange reserves in the world. The willpower of them caught the attention of the world once again.

After the bailout incident of IMF, the citizens formed a new resolution. This brought many changes and the promotion of new industries, such as the service industry, culture, or environment, was spurred. The industries that led South Korea's economic growth are as follows. During the 1970s and the 1980s, the textile industry played a great role in the growth. Korean clothes were selling out to the world like wildfire, and the word 'Made in Korea' was introduced to the global market. From the 1980s to the middle 1990s, the car industry flourished. Cutting-edge products have appeared as South Korea's main ones since the late 1990s: semiconductors, computers, mobile phones, etc.

South Korea's gross national income (GNI) of rose from 87 dollars in 1962 to 12,197 dollars in 1996, and so South Korea entered the so-called 'Ten Thousand Dollar Age.' After shaken temporally during the foreign exchange crisis, its GNI was recovered to 10,841 dollars. in 2000. According to the Bank of Korea, South Korea's GNI was 20,045 dollars in 2007 and increased to 22,708 dollars in 2012.

South Korea has the 11th largest economic scale (787,500,000,000 dollars) in the world on the basis of GDP and the 12th largest trading scale (545,600,000,000 dollars) in the world. South Korea joined the Organization for Economic Cooperation and Development (OECD) in 1996 and made so much progress that it entered the top 10 in the world's main industry fields. Recently, Korean

순위 날	1인당	국민총소득(달러)
1	미국	4만6040
2	영국	4만660
3	독일	3만8990
4	프랑스	3만8810
5	일본	3만7790
8	한국	1만9730

Comparison of per capita national income among countries with population more than 40 millions

economic growth was somewhat dull due to side effects of the global economic crisis. But, the economic growth is noticeable.

For the standard of economic life, South Korea ranked 1st in the number of households using the internet, 1st in the field of information and communications, and 3rd in the number of households with computers. All people of South Korea enjoyed the benefits of the information age. Korean people are doing convenient economic activities. For example, they can buy goods by internet banking at home. Most Korean families own a car. Recently all of Korean people have their mobile phone. In particular, smartphones made by Samsung Electronics are gaining popularity.

Samsumg Electronics.co.ltd and Hyundai Motors

Samsumg Galaxy S

The representative Korean companies' CIs

The followings are chosen as the representative companies of South Korea:

Samsung, LG, Hyundae, SK, Asiana, Doosan Heavy Industries & Construction, CJ Corporation, AMOREPACIFIC Group, Dong A Pharmaceutical Company, Lotte, KT, Korean Airlines, etc. With a thorough service mind, South Korea's companies are doing their best to 'move the hearts of customers.' Korean companies' follow-up services are done so quickly and the staff are so kind that foreigners admired their services.

Exercises

01 Read the following statements, and if true put O between the brackets and if not, put X instead.

2) The president of South Korea idirectly voted by the citizens and limited to a single 5-year term. (   )

2) Moo-Hyun Roh is the only one who was awarded the Nobel Peace Prize among the presidents of South Korea. (   )

3) President Chung-Hee Park achieved South Korea's economic revival called 'Miracle on the Han River.' (   )

4) South Korea received funds to achieve its economic growth from US.

5) The person who has worked as the UN Secretary-General of the United Nations since 2007 is from South Korea. (   )

02 Out of the presidents of South Korea, which one first comes to mind? And why?

03 What is the name of the state-controlled network supported indirectly by viewers via subscription fees? Also state the name of the broadcasting station which targets at overseas Koreans and Korean people who reside abroad.

04 Korean young men have the duty to go to the army when they are 18 years old. What historical event has to do with this?

05 Write all you know about the causes and characteristics of South Korea's economic growth. Also write about how Korean people overcame the financial crisis after South Korea received $57 billion in bailout money from IMF in 1997.

Korean people live to learn, even if they are poor! A Country without Illiterate People

Step 1 Education Fever and Education System

1. Korean people's fever for education

It is commonly said that '*ja sik nong sa* 자식농사 (bring up children)' is most important in everything.

It means that Korean people value education above everything else. In the 1970s South Korea was making a leap towards the goal of economic development. All the people's fever for education was extraordinary. People even in rural areas did everything they could do to send their children to a university and those children achieved academic success in spite of hunger. Public education was prior to private education and school teachers had higher authority over their students. The norms of school life were so sever that all middle and high students wore their uniforms. Since the 21st century, Korean people's fever for their children's education has been more intensifying because of South Korea's continuous economic growth and low birthrate. The private lessons and academies after school are accelerating the fever more.

It is said that these days children in normal families have received special education for the gifted since the time of prenatal education. Korean parents buy expensive books and textbooks to teach their child letters when they are born. These parents have their child learn various arts and foreign

Classroom of 3th grade highschool students 100 days before
taking a College Scholastic Ability Test

languages from kindergarten. Elementary school students go abroad to
learn foreign language every vacation. Middle and high school students
study until midnight at private institutes to prepare for university entrance
examination. Recently there is an increase in the phenomenon where many
women take their children to foreign countries to get them good education
and their husbands are left behind to work in South Korea to pay for their
families to live and study. These husbands are called '*gi reo gi a ppa* 기러기
아빠 (goose father).' It is common that university students go to one or two
countries to learn foreign language before they graduate.

South Korea's popular drama 'Catch a Gangnam Mother' was
broadcasted by SBS in 2007. It is a modern version of the story of
Mencius's mother moving her house 3 times before finding a location that

she felt is suitable for bringing up her child. The main character Min-Joo of the drama moved to the wealthy area of Gangnam to have her child receive the best possible education. The prices of apartments in Gangnam-gu skyrocket because the area belongs to School District 8 whose high schools have a high college acceptance rate of their students. The female parents in the area are called 'Gangnam Mothers.' This shows an example of Korean people's excessive fever for education.

According to investigations conducted by the Ministry of Education and the National Statistical Office (NSO), the total annual cost of private education was estimated at 20 trillion won. The government has carried out every possible policy to decrease the burden of the cost, but the policy is not effective because of parents' hot fever for education.

2. Why study so hard?

Why do Korean people study so hard?

There is a high competition in South Korea because it has a high density of population despite its small area and lack of natural resources. When looking at Korea historically, Korea needed wise agricultural managers as it was an agricultural country. Learning was an essential part to becoming those manager. Korean people developed educational institutions earlier because an agricultural society required literate managers whereas a nomadic society needed warriors and hunters.

There were already educational institutions as early as the Three Kingdom Period. In 372, a state institute for higher education called *tae hak* 태학 (National Confucian Academy) was founded in the Goguryeo Kingdom. In 682, a similar institution named *guk hak* 국학 (National Confucian College) was established by the Silla Kingdom. The Goryeo Kingdom founded a state institution for higher education called *guk ja gam*

국자감 (National University) in its capital Kaegyung (now Kaesong) in 992 and renamed it *sung kyun kwan* 성균관 (National Confucian University). Seong-Gye Lee, who found the Joseon Kingdom in 1392, relocated *sung kyun kwan* to Hanyang (now Seoul), and it was built as the pinnacle of Confucian education system of Joseon in 1398. *Sung kyun kwan* was the matrix of Sungkyunkwan University in Seoul. In the Joseon period there were four classes of society aristocrats, farmers, artisans and tradesmen, and aristocrats (or classical scholars) were in higher position that the other three classes. This created the so-called '*Seon Bi* (classical scholar) Ideology' to emphasize study and respect intellectuals. Even these days teaching is regarded as a good job.

In the late Joseon period, modern education began as missionary schools were opened by Christian missionaries from the West. Today's Yonsei University and Ewha Womans University were founded in those days. Modern education seemed to be regressing because of Japan's policy to obliterate the Korean nation and of the Korean War, but Korean people's fever for education was not lost. After the Korean War, Korean people recognized again that education is a long-range project of the country. The government actively promoted a education policy to cultivate human resources.

Further, Korean people have their own alphabet, called 'hangul 한글.' So, their fever does not easily cool down. Hangel is so simple that it can be mastered easily by anyone. The following two things are related to the fact that the Korean alphabet is easy to learn. One is that South Korea was chosen as a country which has a literacy of 100%. The other is that South Korea has higher educational level than any other countries.

In a word, it is not too much to say that Korean people risk their life to study.

In addition to the above things, the origin of the fever is Korean people's awareness of crisis that they cannot compete against people of other countries without education in the current situation of division of the small country Korea. It is Korean people's education fever that is the momentum of Korean economic growth out of ashes of the Korean War in the 1950s. Korean people are not reluctant to get a loan for their children's education fees. They concentrate more on educating their children because the 21st century is a knowledge economy society where knowledge is money.

The Korean government assigned a large portion of the total budget to education because it recognized the fact that training talented individuals is a driving force of national development. According to 2004's statistics, the rankings of the government's budget allocation are as follows: 1. Economic Development (25.5%), 2. Education (18.5%), and 3. National Defense (16.5%).

3. South Korea's education system

Education system in South Korea is generally comprised of school education (school education), private education, special education and adult education. That is to say, the main track of the system includes six years of elementary school, three years of middle school, three years of high school and four years of university education. There are graduate schools for master's and doctoral degrees. Also, there are kindergartens for pre-school children aged three to five and special education institutions for disabled people.

South Korea's elementary education starts at the age of 6. The compulsory education is until the end of middle school, and its duration is 9 years. High schools are divided into general high schools (including science high schools and foreign language high schools) for students to go to a university and vocational high schools. Most of the people (92.6%)

graduate from high school.

There are 412 higher education institutions (universities and junior colleges) in South Korea in as of 2006. The private institutions have the largest percentage of them: national (46), public (10) and private (356). The percentage gives the big burden of educational fees to people. Nevertheless, in 2006 82.1% of high-school graduates entered university or junior college because of school parents' hot fever for education. The higher education institutions include graduate schools, 4-year universities and 2-year or 3-year junior colleges. The 4-year universities consist of colleges or schools. For example, Seoul National University is composed of 16 colleges and schools: Humanities, Natural Sciences, Business Administration, Engineering, Human Ecology, Liberal Studies, Music, Pharmacy, Social Sciences, Agricultural Life Sciences, Education, Fine Arts, Law, Medicine, Nursing, and Veterinary Medicine. Suppose a person who wants to major in architecture. First, the person finds a university whose cut-off score is satisfied by his or her score. Then, the applicant finds the College of Engineering of the university. Finally, he or she enters the Department of Architecture in the college.

Recently, in South Korea lifelong education and cyber university education are developed well because of the people's higher level of education and of an increase in internet users. The internet enables workers to enter a university, study their major at home and finally obtain a bachelor's degree.

The environment of female education made a revolutionary change. The education for women was overlooked 50 years ago when the tradition of Confucianism was valued. But, both men and women receive the same school education today. Women's college entrance rate is rising greatly as there is an increase in female workers. According to statistics released by the Ministry of Education & Human Resources Development in 2008, the college entrance rate of women was 83.5%.

4. University entrance examination and graduation

University entrance examination

The admission for universities in South Korea is based on the score of College Scholastic Ability Test (CSAT) and high school records. To enter a university, the applicants must satisfy the admission requirements decided by the relevant university. Some universities select students based on the scores of CSAT, an essay test, and an oral test and the document(s) of volunteer activities. So, applicants must collect the admission information of the university they want to enter.

Korean people are so interested in CSAT that they are cautious about visiting the family looking after a child who is a senior in high school. The whole Korean people consider every detail to help examinees in the day of CSAT. The government delays salaried workers' attendance time to reorganize the whole country's driving time lest the examinees arrive late at the test site in the morning on the day. Television stations broadcast the examination process live across the country all day. In a Buddhist temple or a church there were usually found on the day people praying for their children who were taking CSAT. There is also the custom that in the previous day of CSAT examinees eat *yeot* 엿 (a stick of taffy) or *chap ssal tteok* 찹쌀떡 (sticky rice cake) to pass the test.

Entrance and graduation

The Korean school year begins in March.

The school year ends in February of the next year. The entrance ceremonies for kindergartens to universities are held in March. In the entrance ceremonies for new elementary students, there can be seen their family members who are taking celebration pictures. This shows values of Korean people who emphasize their children's education. They celebrate the ceremonies because they think that these ceremony symbolizing the start of school eduction of a family member are one of the events to foster the member to be great. In particular, Korean people place importance on graduation ceremonies over entrance ceremonies because they think that the end is another start. At every graduation ceremony, people graduating are celebrated by, and receive gifts from, their family members and friends from far away. Yellow Prizea flowers are hung over school gates on the day. The graduation ceremonial halls turned into a sea of tears in a time when South Korea was a poor country. In other words, a graduation ceremonial hall became a sad place of separation because poor people graduating should work instead of entering a higher school. Especially, when the juniors in the school sang the graduation song, teachers and students hugged each other and cried in the sadness of separation. These days, today's graduation days are greatly different from those of the 1970s because most graduate students enter a university. On the day, many events are performed on graduation ceremonial halls in a festival mood.

A diploma and a yearbook are granted on the graduation day. The yearbook contains the photographs of graduates, teachers, and school buildings and events that make memories. Korean people keep it because it makes their precious memories forever. A graduation association is organized based on the yearbook. In the graduation ceremonial halls, the graduating people wear a black cap and gown and have their graduation picture taken. Some of graduates put their cap on their parents and take a picture of their parents to reward them for the sacrifice.

Step 2 Study in South Korea

In a few years there has been a rapid increase in foreigners studying in South Korea. This is because foreigners who returned to their country after studying in South Korea have an advantage of getting a job because of the influence of the Korean Wave and of many Korean companies which extended their business abroad. Recently there is opened the exhibition 'Studying in South Korea' hosted by the Ministry of Education every year. The businesses of studying in South Korea are supervised by the National Institute for International Education (NIIED) (http://www.niied.go.kr), an institute directly responsible to the Ministry of Education, Science and Technology. The good side of studying abroad in Korea introduced by this place are like thus.

1. Advantages of studying in South Korea

Advanced country with cutting-edge technology

South Korea boasts a world-class level in the field of information and communication. In particular, South Korea has the highest level of information communication technology (ICT) and mobile communication technology in the world. Most of Korean people use a high-speed internet connection installed at home. Given the fact that South Korea is the powerful country of information technology in the world, foreigners who learn the high technology in South Korea can pave the way for his success in the future.

South Korea's major companies (e.g. Samsung, LG, Hyundai Motor Company, Daewoo Shipbuilding & Marine Engineering, etc.) and their affiliated companies have their factories and agencies in foreign large cities such as Beijing. Foreigners who returned to their country after learning information technologies, such as semiconductor technology, in South Korea have an advantage of getting a job. South Korea's game industry is famous all around the world. Foreigners who major in the following fields led by South Korea in the world will have the opportunity to contribute to the trade between their country and South Korea: movie, music, environmental engineering, fashion design, cosmetics, etc.

For example, there is a Chinese student who finished graduate school in South Korea after learning Korean for two years in his country. He successfully completed a Korean language course at relatively low costs in a university in the countryside of South Korea, and then he entered one of famous universities in Seoul. He is now planning to return to China after working for a company for a few years in South Korea. Because he received job offers from many Korean big companies, he is now wondering about choosing a company for him. His hometown is Qingdao (青島) of Shandong (山东) in China, entered by many Korean companies. He wanted to find a job in a Korean company which has a branch in Qingdao. This is because he can continue to work for the same company even after returning to China.

Low costs of studying in South Korea

Compared with English speaking countries such as US and UK, the costs of studying and living in South Korea are greatly low. It is more appealing for foreigners to study in South Korea because recently the Korean government announced plans of scholarship, dormitory, part-time job and employment after graduation so as to greatly support foreign students studying in South Korea. Generally, school expenses of university include entrance fees and tuition fees. Tuition fees are paid every semester whereas entrance fees are paid only once. Tuition fees differ according to whether the university is located at Seoul or other regions. Further, tuition fees vary according to the student is enrolled in the department of humanities or natural science and engineering. University tuition fees are lower than junior college ones. Information of school expenses can be checked through the website of each university or junior college.

Abundant scholarship system

in South Korea there are various scholarship systems in addition to scholarships for outstanding students. Every university and junior college is making efforts to give benefits of scholarships to foreign students. The method of application for scholarship is on the bulletin board at the university or junior college.

Excellent education environment and faculty

The faculty of universities in South Korea are the teaching staff who have a Ph.D. degree. Many of them have experiences of research in other countries as well as South Korea. Students can obtain an opportunity to attend famous overseas universities, such as the University of Oxford and Harvard University, on an exchange scholarship because universities in South Korea set up a sisterhood relationship with these foreign universities.

Universities have the experimental environment to train technical professionals in cooperation with companies. This is proved by the fact that the South Korean team won the championship consecutively in 'the

International Vocational Training Competition (IVTC).' In 2007 South Korea showed the world's best technology by winning the championship among the 49 IVTC members.

Friendly atmosphere to foreign students in South Korea

Korean people are kind at heart and have a lot of interests in foreign cultures. They have a great passion to learn a new culture. According to the emotion of Korean people who put emphasis on education, they actively help foreign students study in South Korea.

Each university and junior college in South Korea has an office for foreign students. The office offers convenience to them as much as possible. The website of the office helps them register for courses, seek an accommodation (e.g. dormitory, boarding house, etc.) and a part-time job and use a transportation card to save traffic costs.

2. Procedures and test for study in South Korea

There are two ways for foreigners to enter a university or junior college in South Korea.

The first one is the Korean government's invitation to study at a university or junior college in South Korea.

The applicant must satisfy the requirements of the followings to be a state scholarship student: (1) academic results, (2) Test of Proficiency in Korean (TOPIC) and (3) English test.

The second one is to study in South Korea at the applicant's own expense.

Generally, the applicant can obtain information of the admission procedure for the desired university on its website. If the applicant has a valid TOPIC score used as a requirement for the admission, he or she will have an advantage of choosing the desired university or junior college or major. TOPIK aims to evaluate the Korean language skills of non-native Korean speakers and overseas Korean people. The applicants of TOPIK can find information of the date and place of it on the TOPIK website (http://www.topik.go.kr).

3. Introduction to Universities in South Korea

Seoul National University (SNU) was formerly Kyoungsung Imperial University, which was founded by the Japanese colonial government in 1926 mainly for the education of Japanese residents other than for the Korean people. Kyoungsung Imperial University was renamed SNU in 1946 and is South Korea's first national university. SNU has 16 colleges and schools containing 104 departments and is considered as the best university in South Korea. Further, SNU is winning an international fame.

The forerunner of Korea University (KU) was Bosung College, established in 1905. In 1946, Bosung College was renamed KU and grew to

Main gate of Seoul
National University

Logos of the representative Korean universities

the status of university. KU is the representative private university which has shared its fate with the Korean people in Korean history. KU aims on higher education towards globalization based on the national spirit of Korean people and has many traditions of continuing good relationships between seniors and juniors.

Yonsei University originated from Yonhui Junior College founded in 1915 and Severance Medical College whose forerunner was the royal hospital Gwanhyewon opened in 1885, which is the oldest western-style hospital in Korea. The two colleges merged to form Yonsei University in 1957.

Yonsei University has 17 colleges containing 83 departments.

Sungkyunkwan University was formerly *sung kyun kwan*, built as the pinnacle of Confucian education system of Joseon in 1398, the early Joseon period. *Sung kyun kwan* was reopened and named Sunggyungwan College in 1946. The college was renamed Sungkyunkwan University and grew to the status of university in 1953.

The forerunner of Ewha Womans University was Ewha Woman's Junior College, which was established as the first woman's junior college in Korea in 1925. The college originated from Ewha Hakdang, the first girl's school opened in 1886 based on the soul of Christianity. Ewha Womans University has cultivated a wide range of females of talent since 1886.

Korea Advanced Institute of Science & Technology (KAIST), located in Daedeok Innopolis, is the first graduate school-oriented university in South Korea. KAIST aims to cultivate high-quality scientific and technical personnel.

Pohang University of Science and Technology (POSTECH) located in Pohang-si, Gyeongsangbuk-do, operates an industrial-educational cooperation system with Pohang Iron & Steel Co. (POSCO) and Research Institute of Industrial Science & Technology (RIST).

Kyunghee University is famous as College of Oriental Medicine. Hanyang University has a reputation for an engineering college. Chung-Ang University is famous as School of Mass Communication and has produced outstanding entertainers leading the Korean Wave.

Step 3 Career Path and Occupation

Once a phrase called 'Korean people are coming' has come up in the world's mass communication. Foreign businessmen sent to South Korea for business all say, 'Business in Seoul is very flourishing.' Mr. Peter, who came to South Korea as an employee of the Australian Trade Representative said Korean people do not fear danger but rather turn it to their advantage. And, he added as follows:

'Their business style is faster and more flourishing compared to any other country in Asia. I was deeply impressed by the confidence and belief of Korean businessmen who welcome new ideas and chances.'

The business style of Korean businessmen is very straightforward. They are not only very skillful and strong negotiators but also are faithful and humble.

Korean office workers express themselves as the busiest workers in the world. A recent survey of public opinion of male office workers showed that they have so much affection for their work that for them it takes priority over their family. Normally office workers get to their offices before 9 am and work until 6 pm. According to the 2005's report of Organization for Economic Cooperation and Development (OECD), the number of average annual hours actually worked per person in employment in South Korea is 2,351 (the number of average week hours 45.21). That tells us that they work 5 hours more than statuary working hours (40 hours per week). So, Korean people were called the world's most diligent 'worker ants'.

However, recently the aspect of labor markets in South Korea is becoming different. That is because the demands of workers have increased and the awareness of the businessmen has gradually since South Korea continued to have a stable economic growth. As the structure of the economy changes, the number of jobs in the service industry is rapidly increasing whereas the importance of agriculture and fishing in South Korea is drastically decreasing. Recently, there is a sudden increase in the avoidance of 3D occupations (i.e. Dirty, Difficult and

Job interviewees

Dangerous Occupations) by the young generations who have grown up with economic benefits, contrary to the workers of the 1960s and 1970s. Because South Korea's manufactures of products, such as casting products, leather articles, plated wares and dyeing products, suffer from a severe manpower shortage, they recruit foreign workers.

When Korean people choose an occupation, they regard 'safety' as the first, 'income' as the second, and 'benefit' and 'possibility of future growth' as the third. In the past, obedience towards superiors at work was considered as a virtue. It was also thought desirable to work for one company faithfully for a long time. These days, the concept of 'permanent workplace' is weakening as there is an increase in companies that determine the amount of salary and the promotion according to the employees's creativity and ability.

In the 1980s, it was a pride and joy to enter a major company after university. The employment of university graduates became more difficult compared to the past as the number of recruiting candidates for major companies fell because the growth rate of Korean companies slowed by the effects of the bailout from IMF in 1997. These days, Korean young people look overseas to find a job in United Nations (UN) or foreign large companies. They prepare early for it. Many of young people establish a company early with their talents. It is the company that is called a venture company. The popular occupations of young people in South Korea are jobs in the cultural industries, such as music and movie, to display one's originality, rather than in large companies or organizations. However, Korean people still prefer relatively stable occupations such as government officials, doctors, and university professors.

There are a lot of information of employment in South Korea. Universities and junior colleges supply information of employment frequently, carry out an aptitude test for employment, and perform a job counseling role, for their graduates. Further, the government give unemployed people better and cheaper education services for reemployment so that they can work for a company again.

Exercises

01 Read the following statements and if they are right put O between
( ), and if wrong put X

1) Korean people's fervor for education is so high that they usually
depend on public education than private education. ( )

2) In the era of the education of modernization, Yonsei University and
Ewha Womans University were founded by missionaries. ( )

3) The Korean school year begins in March and ends in February of the
next year. ( )

4) Because most of the higher education institutions in South Korea are
private universities and junior colleges, people have a big burden of
educational fees. ( )

5) The compulsory education is the start of elementary school to the
end of middle school, and its duration is 9 years. ( )

02 Write down the main track of South Korea's education system.

03 Korean people's fever for education is very high. Find out the
cause of it, and talk about it comparing it with your country.

04 What is the test to evaluate the Korean language skills of non-
native Korean speakers and overseas Korean people?

05 When Korean people choose an occupation, they regard safety,
income, and benefit and possibility of future growth. What is the
thing which they take most into consideration when choosing a
job? Write it down while comparing it with yourself.

National Character of Loving to Sing and Dance

Step 1 Traditional Culture and Heritage

1. Arirang, *pan so ri and sa mul no ri*

Korean music is roughly categorized into Korean classical music and Western style music.

Korean classical music is defined as traditional music passed down for a long time. Western style music stands for the music expressing Korean people's emotion with Western music introduced to Korea after 1990's.

Korean classical music are sub-categorized into two genres; *jeong ak* 정악 (classical music) enjoyed by royal court and noble people and *min sok ak* 민속악 (folk music) beloved by ordinary people. The representative classical music is *jong myo je rye ak* 종묘제례악 (royal ancestral shrine music). The representative ones of folk music include *min yo* 민요 (folk song), *pan so r*i 판소리 (traditional Korean narrative song) and *nong ak* 농악 (famer's music). There are more than 60 musical instruments used for Korean classical music. Typical string instruments are *geo mun go* 거문고 and *ga ya geum* 가야금, wind instruments *dae geum* 대금 and *tung so* 퉁소, and percussions *buk* 북, *jang go* 장고, *jing* 징 and *kkwaeng gwa ri* 꽹과리.

Arirang is the representative Korean folk song. Korean folk song is an indigenous song and melody expressing people's general sentiment of the days plainly. Arirang sublimates ordinary people's lives into an aesthetics of waiting and resentment. Arirang has various versions by region of origin. The typical three Arirang are Gangwon-do Jeongseon Arirang, Jindo Arirang and Gyeongsang-do Miryang Arirang. Miryang Arirang is very lifting.

Arirang

Arirang, Arirang, *Arariyo*

Crossing over Arirang Pass.

Dear who abandoned me

Shall not walk even ten li before his feet hurt.

Pan so ri is a dramatic narrative song. It can be referred to as a solo opera that a *solo so ri ggun* 소리꾼 (singer) performs *so ri* 소리 (songs), *a ni ri* 아니리 (narration) and *bal lim* 발림 (mimetic gestures) beating out rhythm of a *go su* 고수 (a drummer playing a barrel drum called *buk* 북). The term *pan so ri* is composed of two Korean words 'pan' and 'so ri.' 'Pan' refers to the demonstration of a performer's expertise in front of a large audience. 'So ri' means music. *So ri ggun* tells a story attractively while letting audiences entertain and cry. He often speaks to audiences. When the audiences are excited, they participate in the performance with the sounds and words of encouragement, known as *chu im sae* 추임새, such as 'eol ssu 얼쑤.' *So ri ggun* wears *han bok* 한복 (Korean traditional clothing) and holds *bu chae* 부채 (Korean traditional fan) in his or her hand.

Pan so ri was widely performed in the late Joseon period when ordinary people developed their own culture. *Pan so ri* has been passed down mainly in Jeolla Province where arts have been greatly developed since the old time. *Pan so ri* is divided into two *je* 제 (school of pan so ri). One is *dong pyeon je* 동편제 and the other is *seo pyeon je* 서편제 according to its region, the northeast and southwest Jeolla Province, respectively. The movie 'Seopyonje', directed by Gwon-Taek Im, delivered the joys and

Pung mul no ri (famer's music)

So ri ggun and *go su* performing *pan so ri*

Sa mul no ri (famer's music) playing on four Korean traditional percussions *kkwaeng gwa ri* (small gong), *jing* (large gong), *jang go* (hourglass drum) and *buk* (barrel drum)

sorrows of *pan so ri* performers and received high praise at the Cannes Film Festival in recognition of his efforts to remind us of the unique Korean culture.

This movie activated Korean classical music which had lost its ground against Western music and had been declined. Nowadays, it is commonly shown *pung mul no ri* 풍물놀이 (farmer's music) and *pan so ri* is performed at university towns or popular places for young people. There are creative music genres which mix Korean classical music with popular music. Kim Duk Soo Samulnori's performance and Nanta are included in those new genres. *Sa mul no ri* 사물놀이 means farmer's music played on four Korean traditional percussions *kkwaeng gwa ri* 꽹과리 (small gong), *jing* 징 (large gong), *jang go* 장고 (hourglass drum) and *buk* 북 (barrel drum). KIm Duk Soo Samulnori Team is well known for recreating a new traditional farmer's music combined with Western Jazz music's exciting rhythm. This team already performed their music in foreign countries many times and its performance became the world-level famous event.

Two representative folktales 'The story of Chun-Hyang Seong' and 'The story of Cheong Slim'

2. Folktales and poems

Under the traditional large family system, a grandmother told her little grandchildren a lot of tales. Most of them were passed down orally. It is one of Korean people's precious memories to listen to grandmother's old time stories while eating roast chestnuts on snowy winter nights or lying on a low wooden bench on hot summer nights.

Many of them are of fairy tales about goblin, ghost, or god of mountain or of family conflict. A typical lesson in these old tales is that the good triumphs over the evil. People made efforts to raise their children with the lesson of old tales. Korean people's favorite folktales are '*chun hyang jeon* 춘향전 (The story of Chun-Hyang Seong)', '*kong jwi pat jwi* 콩쥐팥쥐 (Kong-Jwi and Pat-Jwi)', '*shim cheong jeon* 심청전 (The story of Cheong Shim), and '*heung bu wa nol bu* 흥부와 놀부 (Heung-Bu and Nol-Bu)'.

A lot of priceless poetry was created during the Japanese colonial time when Korean people realized the importance of hangeul 한글 (Korean alphabet) and they struggled to use it as much as possible. The representative Korean poet is So-Wol Kim (1903-1934). Korean people remind their hometown and miss a person they love when reading his poems. The following is Korean people's most favorite poem, '*jin dal rae kkot* 진달래꽃 (azaleas)'.

Azaleas

When you feel disgusted at my looking
And you'd leave me
I will let you go without a word
An armful of Azalea flowers of Mount Yak, at Yongbyun
I will pluck and spread on your way to leave
Please lightly and gently tread
The flowers on your way every step after step
When you feel disgusted at my looking
And you'd leave me
I won't let any tear drop fall
Even if I'd rather die

3. Dance and play

The Korean dance and play were originated from harvest ritual of ancient tribes. After completing the ritual, they drank alcohol, sang and danced together. The Korean dance is categorized into traditional dance and modern dance. Traditional dance is sub-categorized into court dance and folk dance. Court dance includes all the dances performed in court ceremonies. There are some court dance such as *jang gu chum* 장구춤 (group dance with double headed drum) and *bu chae chum* 부채춤 (fan dance) which have been frequently performed. One of the popular Korean dances, *hwa gwan mu* 화관무 which literally means

Tal chum (mask dance)

flower crown dance, is a dance borrowing its attire from the traditional court dance. Dancers are elegantly dressed in full court attire and wear crowns beautifully ornamented with beads of five different colors.

Folk dance includes *tal chum* 탈춤 (mask dance-drama), *gang gang sul lae* 강강술래 (circle dance for women), *seung mu* 승무 (monk's dance), and *sal pu ri chum* 살풀이춤 (exorcist's dance). The feature of *sal pu ri chum* is a long white scarf in dancer's hand which is related with Korean people's habit of dancing with holding a scarf when they are exhilarated.

The traditional Korean drama includes *tal chum* 탈춤 (mask dance-drama), *kkok du gak si* 꼭두각시 (traditional puppet play), and *mu dang gut no ri* 무당굿 놀이 (shaman's paly). Tal chum is satirical drama set to music and dance performed by actors wearing masks. One of the famous *tal chum* is *ha hoe tal chum* 하회탈춤 in Andong, Gyeongbuk Province. It mostly deals with the late Joseon period's influential noble men in Andong to satirize and criticize them. The expression of masks are made to show the character's personality effectively. Modern play has been developed since 1950s. 'The Last Empress (in Korean 명성황후 *myeong seong hwang hoo*)' is internationally well known Korean modern musical which received favorable reviews including its play performed on Broadway as well as in Korea. Many Korean modern plays are presented in theaters located at Dongsung-dong, Seoul. This place always offers various performances.

4. Painting, calligraphy and craft

It is presumed thatKorean painting started to develop greatly from the beginning of the Three Kingdom period. The arts of Goguryeo remain in the form of murals in the ancient Goguryeo tombs painted on the walls and the ceilings of burial chambers. The representative ones of murals are *su ryeop do* 수렵도 (hunting scene), *mu yong do* 무용도 (dancing scene) and *pung sok do* 풍속도 (culture scene). The arts of Silla are seen in *cheon ma do* 천마도 (Heavenly Horse Painting) in *cheon ma chong* 천마총 (Heavenly horse tomb). This painting shows the dignity of Silla arts. In the Goryeo period, buddhist painting was flourished. On the other hand, a variety of genre paintings were painted during the Joseon period. The tradition of Korean fine arts was firmly established during this period.

Traditional Korean painting is not colorful and drawn plainly with brush and black ink. As a subjects of the paintings, more human figures were chosen than landscapes. The representative one of Korean traditional paintings is *sa gun ja* 사군자 (four gracious plants) produced by the nobility *yang ban* of the Joseon period. *Sa gun ja* is an ink-and-wash painting featuring four gracious plants the plum blossom, orchid, chrysanthemun, and bamboo. Other popular subject matters in Korean painting are pine tree and tiger. Korean people regard evergreen pine tree as a symbol of steadfast

Two of four gracious plants orchid and bamboo

Genre painting by Hong-Do Kim

Tiger

The caligraphy by Jeong-Hee Kim

loyalty or friendship. For tiger, it is usually depicted in humorous appearance which might be resulted from its popularity as a character of children's story. During the late Joseon period, fairly plenty of paintings were drawn to express the everyday life of the ordinary people, called 'genre paintings.' The greatest master is Hong-Do Kim (pen name: Dan Won). His major works are *seo dan*g 서당 (village school) and *ssi reum* 씨름 (Korean wrestling).

Seo ye 서예 (calligraphy) is another category of arts. Noblemen mainly enjoyed it to cultivate themselves. The most famous calligrapher of the Joseon period was Jeong-Hee Kim. Nowadays, many people write Korean characters instead of Chinese ones, decorating their house with a family motto or maxim calligraphy.

Traditional craft includes *han ji* 한지 (traditional paper) craft, tal, metal craft and *na jeon chil gi* 나전칠기 (lacquer ware inlaid with mother of pearl) as well as ceramics. Korean ceramics are made of so fine clay that Korean ceramic ware feature its high quality and unique colors. Goryoe *cheong ja* 고려청자 (Goryeo celadon), the representative ceramic ware of the Goryeo Dynasty, is well known as the representative Korean artwork to the world. In the Joseon Dynasty, Joseon *baek ja* 조선백자 (Joseon white porcelain) became widely popular which has beautiful simplicity of design. These celadon and white porcelain are glazed pottery of high quality. Ordinary people used earthenware vessels made of red clay without glaze. There were various size of earthenware vessels including jar, pot, and crock. Earthenware restrains the propagation of bacteria and is a breathable container. These functions of earthenware is very suitable for Korean diet because there are many fermented food such as *gan jang* 간장 (soybean sauce), *doen jang* 된장 (soybean paste), kimchi, *mak geol li* 막걸리 (rice wine) which need long-term preservation.

In Icheon and Yeoju, the suburbs of Seoul, are notable for kiln sites. Ceramic museums in these two cities are good for a one-day family picnic

White porcelain and brassware

Jeonju Hanji Culture Festival

Crock

Han ji dolls playing farmer's music

Han ji clothing decorated with Korean words

because people not only can see a variety of ceramics and make ceramics themselves but also can purchase modern ceramics.

Han ji craft is a Korean traditional paper artworks. *Han ji* refers to all varieties of traditional Korean paper made out of mulberry tree bark and one of the commonly used *han ji* is *chang ho ji* 창호지. *Han ji* has tender, durable texture as well as rough fiber which enables color to spread very naturally. With these characteristics, small tray, jewel box, doll and many other artworks can be made of han ji. The leading producer of *han ji* is Jeonju, Jeonbuk Province where Jeonju Hanji Culture Festival is held every year in May.

One of the well known Korean metal craft is *yu gi* 유기 (brassware). Brassware was Korean traditional tableware. It gives off a soft golden gleam and look beautiful. It is scientifically proven that brassware not only kills harmful bacteria and insects and notifies us agricultural chemicals in food by turning black but also generates good mineral. However, brassware should not be treated recklessly because it is rather heavy tableware and easily discolored. So, it is only used for ancestral rites because we are too busy to use it carefully. There is an expression '*an seon mat chum* 안성맞춤 (perfectly fitted)' which derived from the region Anseong, Gyeongi Province where the highest quality of brassware is produced.

5. World Heritage Sites

World Heritage Sites

As of August 2013, UNESCO's World Heritage Sites in Republic of Korea are as follows; (1) Haein Temple Janggyeon Panjeon, the Depositories for the Tripitaka Koreana Woodblocks (2) Jongmyo Shrine (3) Seokguram Grotto and Bulguksa Temple (4) Changdeok Palace Complex (5) Hwaseong Fortress (6) Gochang, Hwasun and Ganghwa Dolmen Sites (7) Gyeongju Historic Areas (8) Jeju Volcanic Island and

Injeongjeon in Changdeok Palace

Dolmen remains

Hwaseong Fortress

Bulguk Temple in Gyeongju

Mount Nam in Gyeongju Historic Areas

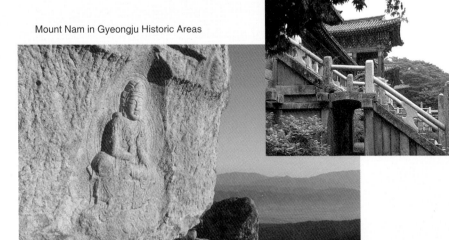

Lava Tubes (9) Royal Tombs of the Joseon Dynasty and (10) Historic Villages of Korea; Hahoe and Yangdong.

The 'Changdeokgung Palace Complex' was established at Seoul in 1405 during the early Joseon Dynasty where kings of many generations managed affairs of state. Compared to other palaces in the same period, the excellence of Changdeokgung is its perfect harmonization with natural setting.

'Hwaseong Fortress' in Suwon, Gyeonggi Province was built by Jeongjo the Great. The king built this fortress to pay respect to his father the Crown Prince Jangheon. The fortress features defensive function of its wall.

Korea's representative temple 'Bulguk Temple' was established in Gyeongju during the Silla Dynasty. Located in Mount Toham in Gyeongju, 'Seokguram Grotto' is said the most elaborate artificial grotto in the world.

'Haeinsa Temple Janggyeong Panjeon' is home to the Tripitaka Koreana, the collection of Buddhist texts engraved on woodblocks. In an appeal to the authority of the Buddha, monks of the Goryeo Dynasty tried to repel Mongol who invaded Goryeo in 1231. They carved the Tripitaka woodblocks for 16 years while seeking the truth. Its outstanding accuracy and superior quality of engraved Chinese characters proves the flourishing buddhism of Goryeo Dynasty and remarkable printing and publishing techniques.

'Jongmyo' is Confucian royal shrines housing the spirit tablet of the former kings and queens of the Joseon Dynasty. Traditional ritual ceremonies linking music and dance still take place there.

In 'Gyeongju Historic Area', a thousand lasting history and culture of Gyeongju, the capital of Silla Dynasty (B.C 57-A.D 935) remains intact. 'go in dol 고인돌 (Dolmen)' is a kind of bronze age's stone grave. It shows prehistoric culture through tombs and evidence of funeral ceremony of two or three thousand years ago. 'Jeju Volcanic Island and Lava Tubes' is listed on the World Natural Heritage

Memory of the World

UNESCO's Memory of the World (MOW) program seeks to protect and preserve world's valuable documents and records. As of August 2013, South Korea holds eleven written records listed in UNESCO's MOW Register: (1) Archives

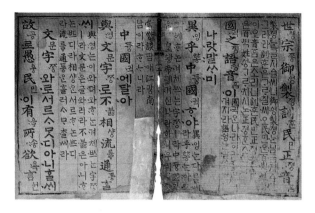

Hae rye Edition of Hunminjeongum

of *Sae ma eul un dong* (New Community Movement) (2) *baek hwa sang cho rok bul jo jik ji sim che yo jeol* (vol. Ⅱ) (the second volume of 'anthology of Great Buddhist Priests' Zen Teachings') (3) *dong ui bo gam* (Principles and Practice of Eastern Medicine) (4) Human Rights Documentary Heritage 1980 Archives for the May 18th Democratic Uprising against Military Regime, in Gwangju, Republic of Korea (5) Ilseongnok (Records of Daily Reflections) (6) *nan jung il gi* (War Diary of Admiral Sun-sin Lee) (7) Printing woodblocks of the Tripitaka Koreana and miscellaneous Buddhist scriptures (8) *Seung jeong won il gi*, (the Diaries of the Royal Secretariat) (9) The Annals of the Choson Dynasty (10) The Humminjeongum Manuscript and (11) *ui gwe* (The Royal Protocols of the Joseon Dynasty.) South Korea is one of the countries with a large number of MOWs in the world. South Korea has the most numbers of MOW in Asia and this indicates that Korean people are deeply interested in moral culture.

'The Hunminjeongum Manuscript' is a book containing explanations and examples of Korean alphabet created by Sejong the Great in 1443. This is also often referred to as the *hae rye* 해례 (commentaries) Edition of Hunminjeongum because the word, Hunminjeongum is written on the cover page of the book as a title. Linguists around the world set a high value on Hunminjeongum Manuscript which logically describes the creating principles of the Korean alphabet and the examples of its use.

'The Annals of the Choson Dynasty' covers 472 years (1392-1863) of the history of the Joseon Dynasty, from the reign of King Taejo, the founder, to the reign of King Cheoljong in chronological order. It consists of 1,893 chapters, 888 volumes which is the most voluminous historical book recorded for the longest time in the world. It is often said encyclopedic annals since it deals with a variety of fields such as politics, diplomacy, society, economics, arts and science, religions, astronomy, geography, music, scientific facts, natural disaster, astronomical phenomena, relations of South East Asia, and daily records from king to humble subject. Especially the authenticity of the contents is highly acclaimed because the annal writer was legally protected whatever he describes. Even a king was prohibited from browsing the annal writer's records.

'*Seung jeong won il gi*' is a diaries recording affairs of state written by the *Seung jeong won* officials, the royal secretariat. The diaries are the authentic historical recordings of the Joseon Dynasty which clearly describes politics, economics, national defense, society, and culture of the period.

'*Bae gun hwa sang cho rok bul jo jik ji sim che yo jeol* (vol. II)', the second volume of 'Anthology of Great Buddhist Priests' Zen Teachings' is acknowledged as the world's oldest movable metal type printing evidence. It was printed seventy eight years prior to the Forty Two-Line Bible created by Johannes Gutenberg in 1455. This book contains the essentials of Zen Buddhism in the late Goryeo period and was printed as a buddhist monks' textbook using movable metal types in July 1377. The publication of this book led to the invention of lithographic writing ink suitable for typography. It has greatly contributed to world printing history. The developed printing technique in the Goryeo Dynasty enabled Sejong the

Great, a king of Joseon following the Goryeo Dynasty to compile a number of books. It is not a mere accident that South Korea has 11 world documentary heritages.

Intangible Cultural Heritage

Intangible heritage means an immaterial but valuable thing which finely expresses the tradition of its society and culture by human creativity. As of August 2013, inscribed South Korean elements on the lists of Intangible Cultural Heritage are as follows: (1) Arirang (lyrical folk song in the Republic of Korea) (2) Falconry, a living human heritage (3) *jul ta gi* (tightrope walking) (4) *tak kyeon* (a traditional Korean martial art) (5) Weaving of *mo si* (fine ramie) in the Hansan region (6) *dae mok jang* (traditional wooden architecture) (7) *ga gok* (lyric song cycles accompanied by an orchestra) (8) *cheo yong mu* (9) *gang gang sul lae* (10) *Jeju Chil meo ri dang Yeong de ung gut* (11) *nam sa dang no ri* (12) *yeong san jae*

Royal ancestral ritual in the Jongmyo shrine and its music

(13) Gangneung Dano Festival (14) *Pan so ri* epic chant, and (15) Royal ancestral ritual in the Jongmyo shrine and its music.

'*jong myo je rye mit jong myo je rye ak* 종묘제례 및 종묘 제례악 (Royal ancestral ritual in the Jongmyo shrine and its music)' means grand national ritual organized by royal family encompassing solemn music, song and dance. The ritual is still practised by clan, Lees of Jeonju, the descendants of Joseon Dynasty in the Jongmyo shrine in Seoul on the first Sunday in May.

'*gang neung dan o je* 강릉 단오제(Gangneung Dano Festival)' celebrates the old shamanistic ritual which is performed on fifth day of fifth month of the lunar calendar to pray for good harvest after finishing rice-planting.

Contemporary Pop Culture

1. Korean Popular Music

'Karaoke are found anywhere there are Korean people.'

To the point of saying that, there are karaoke in places of other countries where many Korean people live. To the eye, people can leap signboards of music businesses, including karaoke, private music school and private piano school, on the streets in South Korea. Korean people enjoy singing competitions in the radio program. Further, there is a Korean song encouraging to sing a song as below.

'If you are not good at singing, you can't have a baby after marriage.'

It is assumed that Korean pop music emerged as modern popular songs spread quickly instead of Korean traditional folk songs. The mass popular song called '*yu haeng ga* 유행가 (music in fashion)' appeared in the Japanese colonial era, but its influence was insignificant. Then, American popular music came in to Korea after the Korean War and was rapidly propagated to Korean people especially to the younger with great impact. Korean popular songs have developed through various genres such as trot, folk music, rock, ballad, dance and hip hop.

In 1950s and 1960s, sorrowful popular music such as trot enjoyed public popularity and two trot singers Mi-Ja Lee and Jeong-Gu Kim received the

Mi-Ja Lee   BoA   Yong-pil Jo

Rain   Girls' Generation

Psy

whole Korean people's love. Lee was named 'the Queen of trot' who would likely to come out once in a century. She released thousands of songs as a representative Korean singer. One of Kim's representative songs *nun mul jeot eun doo man gang* 눈물 젖은 두만강 (Tumen river of tears) expressing the sorrow of displaced people under Japanese dominance is a national song still sung by many Korean people.

Tumen River of Tears

Boatman rowing on the blue Tumen river
My love took the boat and the years flowed on
Where did my love head for?
Missing you! Oh, my love! When will you come?

In the 1970s, young Korean people showed conventional popular culture with an acoustic guitar, jeans and long hair while they yearned for freedom and romance. *Dae hak ga yo je* 대학가요제 (Campus song festival) was a breath of fresh air into the conventional Korean music market in the late 1970s. The most popular singer in the 1980s was Yong-Phil Jo. One of his songs '*dol a wa yo bu san hang e* 돌아와요 부산항에 (Come back to Busan Port)' expresses Korean people's sorrow about their history. This song stirred a boom of Korean Japanese people's visit to South Korea.

When techno, one of electronic dance music, emerged in the 1990s, teenage-hip-hop singers appeared in Korea. Singers of the so-called X generation brought big revolution in 70 years of Korean music history. As the song '*nan a ra yo* 난 알아요 (I know)' by the group 'Seo Taiji and Boys' had enormous influences on music genres of rap and dance music and gained sensational popularity. Two songs released in 1995, '*jal mot doen man nam* 잘못된 만남 (failed love)' by Geon-Mo Kim and '*nal gae il eun cheon sa* 날개 잃은 천사 (an angel who lose its wings)' by Lula, recorded the highest record sales in the 1990s. In these days, the reggae genre which has quick rhythm and powerful dance became young people's music and are creating a greate sensation.

Since 2000, Korean singers has aggressively entered the music business in the world market. Singers 'Rain' and 'BoA' are representative examples of the entrance. First of all, Rain entered Hollywood and was chosen as one of the 100 most influential people in the world by TIME Magazine. The total amount of his income from performances, advertisements and modelling is tens of billions of won whose economic value exceeds a small company. Also, the brand value of BoA is estimated a trillion won. She is so famous as a dance music singer that she was introduced as 'Star of Asia' in the textbook of UK.

Since the middle 2000s, the word 'K-pop (an abbreviation of Korean pop or Korean popular music)' prevailed in the world after Korean popular music was started to be enjoyed by foreigners. It is the music of idol groups whose members sing and dance together that mainly arouse great sensation among the world's young people in the K-pop. These groups are divided girls group, such as 'Girls' Generation' and '2NE1' and boys group including 'Big Bang', '2PM' and 'Super Junior.' The characteristics of their music are upbeat rhythm and easy-to-sing-melody. Five to ten members of them with handsome appearance and sensual fashion style entertain people with their splendid dances. This visual pleasure is very huge compared to Western pops.

In 2012, there was a milestone in Korean music history. It was a song 'Gangnam Style' sung by Psy. His horse-riding dance was passionately enjoyed together by people all over the world although they do not understand others' language. The music video of the song gained huge popularity within a few months after it uploaded onto YouTube and spread via SNS. It ranked No.1 on the Billboard and hit more than 1 billion views on YouTube which set an amazing record beyond anyone's imagination titled as 'Most-viewed YouTube Video.' Psy's two songs 'Gangnam Style' and 'Gentleman' have exciting and impressive factors such as addictive melody that everyone want to sing along, spectacular stage effects, and funny dance. Now, Psy is a world singer beyond K-pop.

As shown in the Psy's case, Korean pop music moves world people as well as domestic ones. The current pop music reached an art form reflecting the its time, but not just an entertainment to simply listen and enjoy. The trend of popular music is not led by teenagers and the 20s and music fields for every generation, including elementary school students and the elder, are growing with the popular music. There are performances such as B-boying accompanying powerful dances and fast beat that teenagers and concerts consisting of old pops for the middle aged people.

Recently, Korean operas which combine Western classical music with Korean traditional music are popular. Korean Operas, such as '*hwang jin i*' and '*Shim cheong*', which are adaptations of Korean classical stories, received high reputation in Korea as well as other countries. These operas captivate an audience with many things to see such as beautiful *han bok* 한복 (Korean traditional apparel) and clean motions of Korean traditional dance to help the audience understand the Korean culture.

The Korean people's passion for music created the world's only 'Song Island' in Nami Island near Seoul in 2003. This island is decorated with hand-printings, busts and monuments of song of singers who encouraged Korean people during national crises. There are many facilities including an archive where people can appreciate musics of the 1920s to now and theaters.

2. Movies and dramas

If the flower of public culture is music, the fruit of public culture can be

Korean TV dramas '*dae jang geum*' and '*goong*'

Korean movies 'Welcome to Dongmakgol' and 'Friend'

movie.

Movies contain national and contemporary characters of a country. In recent years Korean movies have been notably developed to stand shoulder to shoulder with Hollywood movies.

It was the early 1900s when the first Korean film was publicly screened. However, Korean movies could not be shine under the circumstance that people made ends meet after the Japanese colonial era and Korean War. Korean movies started to improve after Korean economic boom in the 1970s. The era of public commercial film was triggered by two movies, 'Love Me Once Again (1968)' and 'The Hometown of Stars (1974)', which gained huge popularity. The development of Korean movies was suspended by the appearance of Television and import of foreign films, but they started qualitative advancement in the late 1980s. The movie 'The General's Son (1990)' set a record of the most highly-attended film in South

Korea in 1990. Another movie directed by Kwon-Taek Im, 'seo pyon je (1993)' taking pan so ri as its theme passed the 1 million viewers mark and was exported to other countries. Then, three movies 'Swiri (1998)', 'Joint Security Area (2000)', and 'Friend (2001)' were consecutively gained tremendous popularity and acquired a favorable reputation from other countries including Southeast Asian countries as well as South Korea. A noted Korean director Kwon-Taek Im made many films taking Korean culture as their theme such as 'chun hyang jeon' and won the Best Director Award at Cannes for 'chwi hwa seon'.

South Korea's movie boom change Korean people's preference of movie from foreign films to Korean films. Since 2000s, Korean films have highly advanced thank to diverse themes and new techniques of young directors.

Movie 'Masquerade'

More than 10 thousands people watched Korean movies 'sil mi do (2004)' and 'tae guk gi: (Brotherhood of War) (2004)' as well as 'My Sassy Girl (2001).' That means that one out of five South Korean people watched these movies. The expression 'the most Korean, the most international' was proved by big hits of two Korean movies 'King And the Clown (2005)' and 'Masquerade (2012).'

In these days, many events such as Busan International Film Festival are frequently held in South Korea. Korean films are not just a thing to watch but also play an important role in the export of 21th century's cultural industry due to the effect of 'hal lyu' (the Korean Wave), as Korean dramas and online games do. There are so many multiplexes such as CGV and Megabox in South Korea that people can spend a full day in one building with abundant things to see and enjoy. It became a cultural attraction for young people because these movie theater complexes provide shopping places as well as multiple screens.

The popularity of Korean TV dramas is tremendous as much as that of Korean movies. South Korea's drama '*dae jang geum*' produced by MBC in 2003 is based on the true story of Jang-Geum, who achieved a success five hundreds years ago in the Joseon period. It is an interesting story of a woman who lived in the hierarchical society which was rarely influenced by women. The story is as follows. Jang-Geum is from the lowest class. She starts to work in court kitchen to become the best royal cook. She is appointed as the king's first female physician against other male physicians. Finally, she obtains the title '*dae jang geum* 대장금', which literally means the Great Jang-Geum. The fruits of this drama are to newly review the Korean royal court cuisine and traditional medicine and to remind its value. It was a successful drama to help the Korean Wave secure its position as a leading culture in China and Southeast Asia. The following is the theme song lyric of the drama.

Onara

Onara onara aju ona
Ganara ganara aju gana
Nanani Daryeodo mot nonani
Aniri daryeodo aninone
Heiya diiya heiyanaranino
Ojido moyhana daryeogana

<English Translation>
If asked to come, did he really come?
If asked to leave, did he really leave?

254

Even after waiting for endless days, we couldn't get together

No, no, it's no

He-i-ya di-i-ya heiyanaranino

Darling, if you can't come

Please take me instead

Another drama 'goong 궁 (Princess Hours) (2006)' followed the popularity of 'dae jang geum' is based on the imaginary world where the Joseon dynasty still continues in Korea. Besides the interesting episodes of royal family, plentiful feasts to the eye including royal costumes and manners were other elements of its popularity. In January 2007, the official poster of 'goong' was released on the main page of Yahoo (http://yahoo. com). The article said DVDs of Korean dramas including 'goong' and Korean films had a tremendous popularity.

3. Cultural space and Nanta

Recently there is an increase in companies which conduct a five-day workweek.

People who enjoy cultural activities during the weekend are also increasing. It is possible to appreciate exhibitions and performances at one site such as National Folk Museum, as well as Sejong Arts Center and Seoul Arts Center in Seoul. National Museum of Modern and Contemporary Art, located in Gwacheon, focuses on fine arts, and it does not present plays but also holds exhibitions of photographs and crafts all year around. Ma-roo, a small theater for teenagers, is located in Myeong-dong in Seoul. It offers programs to learn rap and hip-hop and a place to hold dance competition and birthday party for free.

If you want to experience Korean folk culture, visit Korean Folk Village in Yongin-si, Gyeonggi Province. The village rebuilt the 500-hundred custom and traditional culture of Joseon period. It is used not only for the location of filming and drama but also for the place to learn and experience traditional Korean culture for foreigners. Every region holds festivals with regional products or intangible cultural assets seasonally.

One of the famous performances is 'Nanta' performed at the theater in Jeong-dong, Seoul. The word *nan ta* 난타 means 'randomly hit and beat.' It is a non-verbal performance which comically portrays happenings in a kitchen with Korean traditional *sa mul no ri* 사물놀이 (traditional percussion quartet) rhythm to enjoy regardless of sex or age. It is already well known to people all around world because anyone who do not understand Korean can enjoy this non-verbal performance. The fast and energetic performance is so exciting that audiences automatically dance with their shoulders.

'Nanta' is the representative cultural attraction designated by Korean Tourism Organization. Visit the website http://nanta.i-pmc.co.kr if you want to see the details of it.

Step 3 Korean Wave and Korean culture

Since the 21th century, Korean pop culture has internationally caught popularity as names of *hal lyu*, 한류 (Korean pop fever or Korean Wave) and K-pop. These names started to be used when Korean music, dramas and movies were popular in China.

After Korean drama '*sa rang i mweo gil lae* 사랑이 뭐길래 (What Is Love All About)' was broadcasted in the prime time hour of China Central Television (CCTV) in 1997, it was rerun due to its amazing popularity. '*mok yok tang jip nam ja deul* 목욕탕집 남자들 (Bathhouse Guys)' and '*bo go ddo bo go* 보고 또 보고 (See and see again)' recorded the highest viewing rate subsequent to '*sa rang i mweo gil lae*'. The word '*hal lyu*' was first used by Chinese press in 1999 when a concert in China was held by Clon, who is South Korean dance music duo and sang 'Kungtari Shabara' in 1999.

In 2004 Korean drama 'Winter Sonata' was broadcasted in Japan, booming with unprecedent popularity and the main actor Yong-jun Bae became a hero of Japanese women. They visited Nami Island where the drama was shot. After a Korean drama 'Autumn in My Heart' was run in Taiwan, the main actor Seung-Heon Song's popularity soared and 'Seung-Heon coffee' and 'Seung-Heon T-shirt' became hot items.

The craze for Korean Wave delivered to Korean movies. The advantages of Korean movie are to share beautiful scenery and a warm heart of Korean people shown in family culture with everyone in the world. 'My Sassy Girl', *Tae guk gi*: Brotherhood of War', 'Friend' and 'Swiri' were very popular in Asia. As Korean actors and actresses such as Dong-Geon Jang, Byung-Heon Lee, Na-Ra Jang and Ji-Hyeon Jeon became Korean wave movie stars, their old movies were exported. This phenomenon gave Asian countries the confidence that their movie can compete with Hollywood blockbusters and showed a solution of the problem.

In recent days, the Korean Wave is spread out to Egypt and East Europe as well as Central and South America. Germany declared the 'Year of Korea 2005' and showed Korean movies. The reason why the Korean Wave has the limelight from all over the world is considered as follow.

First, Korean popular culture have excellent marketability and high techniques to deal with mass media. For example, the background scenes of Korean music videos, dramas and movies are very beautiful. Further, OSTs show a high standard of skill to touch people's emotion because they are matched well with scenes of them.

Second, the Korean dramas are easily emphasized by anyone. They make viewers warmhearted because they contain the Korean's kind-hearted national character like love or filial duty. It is the contents of them that are quickly absorbed by Asian people who have the same polite family culture, filial duty, and child rearing method as Korean ones.

Third, Korean Wave has its unique color which is created by combining the positive things of America's advanced culture with South Korean origin sentiments. For instance, there are energetic dance accompanying backdancers, colorful costume and stage in Korean popular music to satisfy people's various needs.

Finally, Korean actors and actresses' handsome appearance and personality, sensuous fashions and their good acting play a key role in the spread of Korean Wave to the world. The power of Korean Wave affects various areas: singers' albums, performances and T-shirts, actors' photographs, magazines, fashion, games, food tourism, cosmetics and plastic surgery. The Korean Wave became an incidence to make headway into overseas markets of Korean culture. Korean language classes opened in colleges and private institutes are crowded with foreign students. According to the materials of Korean Ministry of Culture in 2012, the number of students in 'King Sejong Institute' were sharply increased from 17 branches, 3,971 students in 2008 to 60 branches, 23,709 students in 2011. The craze for the Korean Wave and K-pop is sublimated into 'an international interest in the whole culture of Korea', such as Korean food, Korean traditional culture, pure art, publishing and Korean language. For example, the novel 'Please Look After Mom' written by Kyung-Sook Shin was published in English version and ranked No. 10 in the Amazon's Best Fiction Books of the Year. The sketchy history of Korean Wave are as follow.

Korean Wave 1.0 (1995-2005)
Drama, movie and music (mainly visual contents like dramas)
China, Taiwan, Japan and Southeast Asia

Korean Wave 2.0 (2006-2011)
K-pop, drama and movie (mainly K-pop and idol stars)
Asia, America and some European countries

Korean Wave 3.0 (2012-)
Overall Korean culture
All over the world

The more primary reason than above four things can be found from the ethnicity of Korea. That is, Psy's 'Gangnam Style' moved people all over the world not only because of Korea's economic strength and techniques but also because of ethnicity passed down long time ago. According to the Chapter of Dongyi in the Book of Wei, the Records of the Three Kingdoms which describes

Korean people from the perspective of Chinese, 'Korean people enjoy singing and dancing.' It tells about Korean people's ethnicity with full of '*sin myeong* 신명 (excitement, gay, pleasure, etc.).' When Korean people drink alcohol while having a meal, they enjoy provoking merriment with humming or beating a rhythm with spoon. If that is not enough to enjoy, they go karaoke and loosen up.

Where does this unchanged sin myeong with full of joy come from? You may find it from the beauty of mother nature. There are four seasons in Korea. So, Korean people sing human and nature, seeing colorful flowers in spring and falling leaves in autumn. People naturally sing a song for beautiful nature because Italian people in the Mediterranean climate are called those who are also good at singing.

Sin myeong is also found in agricultural lifestyle. Farmer's music was developed from Korean people's rice transplanting. All villagers cooperated while hitting *buk* 북 (barrel drum) and *kkwaeng gwa ri* 꽹과리 (small gong) and encouraging themselves to try to enjoy their work. Sa mul no ri came from Farmer's music. When someone who were excited about cheerful rhythm of percussions exclaimed, "*sin myeong na ge no ra bo se* 신명나게 놀아보세 (Let's have real fun!)," spectators followed the sa mul no ri team and extemporally danced all together. This is different from Western style. It is difficult for spectators to follow the flashy dance moves accompanying beat music extemporally. Korean artistic entertainment culture has 'communal tendency that anyone can easily enjoy the rhythm.' Numerous K-pop fans sing together along with singers and enthusiastically enjoy it.

Now, South Korea needs a high quality policy for Korean wave to meet consumers' needs. It is necessary to make dramas to introduce better Korean tradition. Korea should provide various textbooks to learn Korean language and culture more easily. It is essential to cultivate capable person to translate Korean into other language exactly when Korean public culture is exported. Also, It is important to hold Korean culture fair and to invite its participants to help them perceive Korean culture through Korean Wave correctly.

Exercises

01 Read the following explanations. If they are right, put O in the brackets next to them. If they are wrong, put X instead.

1) Korean people move their body to their rhythm without saying because they like dancing rather than singing.

2) *Sa mul no ri* is farmer's music played on four Korean traditional percussions *kkwaeng gwa ri, jing, jang go* and *buk*.

3) Korean traditional painting is not colorful and drawn plainly with brush and black ink.

4) One of the representative Korean ceramics is 'Goryeo *cheong ja* (Goryeo celadon)' and it is well known to all over the world.

5) One of the Memory Of the World, 'The Annals of the Choson Dynasty' is recording of one thousand year history of Silla.

02 What is the name of one of the representative Korean folk song which sublimates ordinary people's lives into an aesthetics of waiting and resentment?

03 Recite the subject matters of *sa gun ja*. And describe other matters Korean people frequently paint.

04 Recite UNESCO's World Heritage Sites in Republic of Korea as much as you know.

05 Introduce one example of Korean pop music, drama and movie which brought Korean wave, respectively and share the impressions of them.

The 1988 Seoul olympics and Cheering Heat in the 2002 FIFA World Cup Korea/ Japan

Step 1 Taekwondo and Soccer

1. Taekwondo

History

Have you ever seen a scene where a person with a white uniform and a black belt kicked?

Taekwondo is one of the representative national sports in Korea. Its history goes back to 2000 years ago and originated from the traditional martial arts of the ancient kingdom. An illustration of Taekwondo can be found in mural paintings that appear on the ceiling of *mu yong chong* 무용총 (the Tomb of Dancers), one of Goguryeo's loyal tombs, built in Tong-kou area of Manchuria.

The Korea Taekwondo Association was founded in 1973 and the World Taekwondo Federation (WTF) in 1973. Taekwondo was chosen as a demonstration sport in the 24th Seoul Olympic Games in 1988. After it was adopted as an official Olympics entry in the 26th Sydney Olympic Games, it became an internationally certified sports spreading throughout the world.

The global population of Taekwondo is estimated as 70 million. WIT has 5 regional organizations and 192 member countries in as of 2010 and supervises international matches: the Asian Takewondo Union (ATU, 41

Demonstration of taekwondo

countries), the Europe Taekwondo Union (ETU, · 48 countries), the Pan American Taekwondo Union (PATU, · 42 countries), the African Taekwondo Union (AFTU, · 40 countries), and the Oceania Taekwondo Union (OTU, · 11 countries). The basic rules of Taekwondo to train the body and mind are applied equally worldwide. Two framed flag of South Korea and the relevant country are hung on the front wall of every Taekwondo studio in the world. All masters instruct their trainees by giving orders in Korean to spread the spirit of Taekwondo through out the world.

Exercise and rank

Taekwondo exercises the whole body, and it is a martial art to defend oneself and attack his opponent with bare hands and feet only. Because Taekwondo aims to train the body and mind and promote orderly behavior through practices, it prohibits trainees to use unnecessary violence.

In Taewondon there are 1 white belt, 6 colored belts and 1 black belt related to *dan geup je do* 단급제도 (the rank system) showing the proficiency of trainees. The belts are tied round the wearer's waist. Each colored belt level is called *geup* 급 and the black belt *dan* 단 (degree), as follows: (1) white belt (no rank), (2) yellow belt (10th and 9th geup), (3) green belt (8th and 7th geup), (4) blue belt (6th and 5th geup), (5) purple belt (4th and 3rd geup), (6) red belt (2nd and 1st geup), and (7) black belt (1st to 9th dan). For example, the white belt represents the beginner who does not have previous knowledge of Taekwondo.

Taekwondo has been developed as an martial art to protect the country, and hence it is trained by young men who enter the army. Because these days Korean people have fewer children, they tend to be overprotective to their children. People have their children start to learn Taekwondo as a child, so as to stop being overprotective towards their children and develop their children's independence and endurance. It can be frequently found that cute boys wearing a white a Takewondo uniform walk in the street between houses. Korean people do not only have the pride that Takewondo is a Korean national sport but also love it.

2. Soccer and the 2002 FIFA World Cup

Korean people and soccer

Most Korean males like soccer.

According to Gallup Korea's survey in 2004, soccer is Korean people's most favorite sport. Soccer is a masculine sport and can be enjoyed with a ball at any place. It has been loved for a long time.

It is said that soccer was introduced by the crew of a British warship anchored at Incheon Harbor in 1882. He gave a soccer ball to Korean people. The Korea Football Association (KFA) became a member of the Fédération Internationale de Football Association (FIFA) in 1948. Korean soccer has had a huge development with its economic growth since the Korean soccer team went to the 14th London Olympic Games in 1948. The craze for soccer was intensified when the Korean Super League was launched in 1983. The Korean team made a splendid achievement of going to the semifinals of the 2012 FIFA World Cup in South Korea.

Why did South Korea become a strong force in world soccer although it had a shorter history of soccer than Western countries? Soccer is originally a sport which is advantageous to Western people who have long legs and a strong strength and endurance built by eating meat. Nevertheless, the reason why Korean soccer is strong can be found in Korean people's dispositions. So to speak, they have hot temper that enables them to fight against injustice and desire for winning. They refuse to give up because they get up again although they fall. The strong fighting spirit and willpower enabled them to overcome their physical weaknesses.

Also, teamwork is an important key to victory because soccer is a team sport. Korean people have trained a mind of concession and cooperation while maintaining family communities for a long time. Their community spirit has already been proven by the atmosphere of cheering the Korean soccer team that participated in the 2012 FIFA World Cup. Many foreign media praised the sight of cheering Korean people who united into one, and said, 'Korean people are the only ones who can become one to cheer for their national team.' Korean people have a sense of ethnic community who shout themselves hoarse cheering for the Korean team even if they postpone their businesses. So, it can be said that soccer is advantageous to Korean people because of dispositions.

The schoolyard of schools in South Korea are always open to the public.

The local residents organize a morning soccer club to enjoy playing soccer and become close friends naturally. In South Korea, the school gates are not controlled and there is no need to pay money to use the schoolyard.

Recently soccer fan groups were organized spontaneously through internet networks. The representative one is 'Red Devils.' The group created a new cheering culture. Its members wearing red clothes made a more passionate atmosphere while striking *kkweng ga ri* 꽹과리 (small gong) and *jing* 징 (large gong) every game. Their unique cheering followed the Korean team whenever it plays a game.

The 2002 FIFA World Cup Korea/Japan and Cheering Heat

The 2002 FIFA World Cup, co-hosted by Korea and Japan, was the first FIFA World Cup held in Asia. In the 2002 FIFA World Cup, the Korean team achieved impressive results, making it into the round-of-sixteen and finally creating the legend of advancing to the semifinals. As a result, South Korea became the first country whose team went on to the semifinals of the FIFA World Cup in all countries, excluding European and South American countries. Since then, South Korea has been a strong force in the world soccer.

The cheering heat, Korean people's 'Red Color', of the Sangam World Cup Stadium was particularly impressive. Korean people wearing red clothes with the Korean flag in their hands cheered the Korean team so enthusiastically that other countries misunderstood that the Korean government had told them to do it. The whole Korean people wore red clothes to join the cheering of 'Red Devils' as if with one accord. In those days, Korean people at home and abroad wore red clothes and enjoyed singing '*dae ha min guk* 대한민국 (the Republic of Korea)', the fight song for the Korean team. That is to say, the sports festival displayed Korean people's sense of family community sense. It was without parallel in the

People cheering Korean soccer team at the Seoul Plaza in 2002 FIFA World Cup Korea/Japan

world history of soccer.

There is the 2002 World Cup Memorial Museum in the Sangam stadium, Seoul. The museum has a lot to see: Korean soccer history, soccer information, cyberspace to enjoy a soccer game, and a corner to print out a composite photograph of the members of the Korean soccer team and the visitor's face. It is also a tourist attraction to visit with children.

Sports and Leisure Culture

1. The 1988 Seoul Olympics

The 24th Olympic Games were held in Seoul in 1988.

It was the second Olympic Games held in Asia which 160 nations participated in. The media of each country highly praised that South Korea successfully held the Olympic Games even though it was a divided country.

The official mascot of the Seoul Olympic Games was 'ho do ri 호돌이', which was designed as an amicable Amur Tiger. The name of mascot is a compound word of 'ho' derived from 'ho rang i 호랑이 (tiger)' and 'do ri 돌이 (a diminutive suffix for boys).' The name was chosen because Korean people since old times had thought that tigers are friendly rather than scary. The theme song of the Seoul Olympics was 'Hand in Hand.' After this song was sung by the group 'Koreana' at the opening ceremony of the Olympic Games, the album including it became the world's best-selling one among those which were made by Asian singers. The song reached No.1 in the charts of 17 countries, such as Hong Kong, Japan, and European countries including West Germany after the Olympic Games because it was picked as one of the most refined and wonderful song in the history of the theme song of Olympics.

In the 1988 Seoul Olympics, South Korea won 12 gold medals and

Opening ceremony of 1988 Seoul Olympic Games
Hodoli the mascort of 1988 Seoul Olympic Games and its emblem

placed 4th in the final medal standings. At the Olympics, Korean athletes made outstanding achievements in marathon, archery, wrestling, judo and handball. There is Gi-Jeong Sohn, the eternal idol of Korean people, in marathon which is considered the centerpiece of the Olympics. Under the Japanese control, in 1936 Sohn participated in the 11th Berlin Olympics and became the first Korean to win the gold medal in marathon. In 1992, Young-Cho Whang won the gold medal in the marathon race in the 25th Barcelona Olympics. In South Korea there are recently small and big marathon races entered not only by marathon runners but also by office workers, housewives and children. These races have become events of health, fitness and leisure for the people. For example, the popular family movie 'Malaton (2005)' reflects the social atmosphere. It is an impressive movie where a woman relentlessly trained her mentally disabled son as a marathon racer.

2. Professional Sports

A long time ago, there were no Western sports in Korea. Folk games or

Movie 'Running Boy'
Yeong-Jo Hwang, a marathon
gold medalist

sports, such as tug of war, Korean wrestling, archery and Taekwondo, enabled young people to train their body and mind. Most of modern sports were introduced by foreign missionaries in the early 20th century. Amateur players have turned professional since professional sports were introduced to South Korea in the 1970s.

Ssi reum 씨름 (Korean wrestling) was a folk sport, and its tradition has been inherited through a system of professional sport. In old times, young men of two neighboring towns had a ssi reum match on festive days such as *dan o* 단오 (Fifth Day of the Fifth Lunar Month) and *chu seok* 추석 (Harvest Moon Festival). The match usually took place in a ring of sand, and the first person to touch the ground with any part of the body other than the feet lost the match. The winner was called '*jang sa* 장사 (the strongest man)' and awarded an ox as a prize. An ox was Korean people's most valuable possession because Korea was an agricultural country in those days. The winner enjoyed his victory while triumphantly riding the ox around the ring. Man-Gi Lee, titled *cheon ha jang sa* 천하장사 (the strongest man under heaven) is the most famous ssi reum player in South Korea. Ho-Dong Kang is a famous host of entertainment programs broadcasted by television networks. He used to a famous ssi reum player.

In the 1970s, high school baseball leagues were popular

Ssireum, Korean style wrestling

in South Korea. The Korea Professional Baseball started in 1982 with the participation of six teams: MBC Chungyong (Seoul), Lotte Giants (Busan), Samsung Lions (Daegu), OB Bears (Daejeon), Haitai Tigers (Gwangju), and Sammi Superstars (Incheon). A seventh team was founded in 1986 and an eighth in 1989. Seung-Yeop Lee and Chan-Ho Park are famous Korean baseball players who played in the Japanese and US major leagues respectively.

Korean people think of Se-Ri Park whenever they hear the word golf. Just until she appeared, golf was not popular amongst Koreans. Korean people especially like Sae-Ri Park because they remember her barefoot fighting spirit displayed in the 1998 U.S. Women's Open. When Park hit the golf ball to drive on the final hole at a sudden-death playoff, it landed on a slope next to a pond.

Se-Ri Park in the 1988 u.s. Women's Open

She took her shoes and socks off to hit the ball. Her strong willpower not to give up gave a hope to Korean people who were being forced to suffer by the final crisis after South Korea received the bailout money from IMF in

1997. Golf is now so generalized that elementary school students learn it. Further, a fourth of the world's female golfers are Korean.

3. Leisure culture

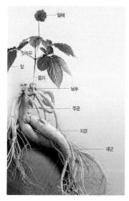
Korean ginseng

Korean people's health consciousness

In sam 인삼 (ginseng)! All Korean people know that it is a herbal tonic.

In the past, a six-year old Goryeo *in sam* was considered as a cure-all. Of course, the mysterious efficacy of in sam is scientifically proved today.

In old times, Korean people preferred herbal medicine prescribed by traditional Korean medical doctors when their health failed or to manage their health. In addition to herbal tonics, they relied on acupuncture, a therapy of traditional Korean medicine, instead of a surgical operation. Today, they still tend to depend on traditional Korean medicine when they cure ill-defined diseases, chronic diseases or geriatric diseases despite the development of modern medicine.

There has been a great advance in traditional Korean medicine. Many universities, including Kyunghee University, have produced traditional Korean medical doctors, held the International Exhibition on Oriental Medicine to spread traditional Korean medicine abroad, and made studies on it. There is a great interest in hand acupuncture, a treatment with acupuncture applied to hand for general diseases of the body. This is because people think that they can keep their health once they learn a few simple tips of it.

Nowadays, many people improve their health by exercise rather than herbal tonics. You can frequently see people jogging in the morning. As car drivers continue to increase, there is an increase in people who jog to prevent a lack of exercise. You can find members of many jogging clubs on the terrace land by the Han River. If you run on the jogging paths along the Han River, you can feel refreshed because of a cool braze from the river.

As the number of companies introducing the five-day work week increases, people are so interested in leisure life that the compound word 'leports' of leisure and sports is generalized. You can see easily young people who enjoy windsurfing in the Han River of Seoul or off the coast of

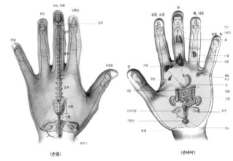

Traditional acupuncture
Hand acupuncture and its points

Incheon on weekends. The ski resorts in Mount Seorak are crowded with people every winter. Because the Yongpyeong Ski Resort has a cold snowy winter weather, it has been a place representing winter leports.

Hiking is an exercise and hobby enjoyed by the most people in South Korea. Because there is a gently rolling mountain anywhere in Korea, Korean people feel snug as if they were cuddled up in the mother's arms when they see the mountain. When they are in a desert or a plain, they get unobstructed, scenic views of it but feel empty inside and uneasy. Because of their heart safely enfolded in the gently rolling mountain, they remind themselves of the meaning of life while thinking that the mountain is a place in their heart. Recently with the expression 'a mountain is calling us', many Korean people go to a mountain or a mountain stream at holidays as if they were hikers. Those who spent their childhood in the countryside want to go to a mountain because of homesickness.

Climbing is a hobby which has greatly spreaded into South Korea since it was industrialized in the 1970s. Because of its rapid economic growth accelerating urbanization, there has been an increase in the stuffiness of apartments as a residential space, and in phenomena of lack of exercise and eye strain due to each family's use of car(s) and computer(s). As societies grow more complex, people suffer more from various stresses and modern diseases. Because of these factors, people climbing a mountain continue to increase. Mount Bukhan or Mount Gwanak in Seoul is crowded with mountain climbers on weekends. Since the 1990s, hobby groups such as 'Climbing Club' have become more active and the climbing population has grown. The activities of expert climbers are so superior that there are people who conquered the Himalayan Mountains, called the 'Roof of the World'. Recently, there have appeared groups of young people who walk all over South Korea feeling the sadness of the division of Korea into South and North with love for their land.

People say, 'There are no bad people who like mountains'. When they go to a mountain, they become humble as they realize the feebleness of humans in front of nature. If you want to make good Korean friends, set up a tent and camp with them in a mountain. You will become their lifelong friends if you use stones as a pillow and the vast sea of brightly shining stars as a blanket. It means that through mountains you can know the beautiful nature of Korea and the true hearts of Korean people.

Korean people go to *no rae bang* 노래방 (karaoke) to relieve their stress

People climbing up the mountain

and enjoy their leisure. When *no rae bang* appeared in the 1990s, they became an instant success. After work, co-workers or friends sing all their favorite songs, relieve their stress and increase their bond. They hold a household party and a family meeting in no rae bang. They choose any of songs for children to elderly people from the no rae bang song list. No rae bang is a new space for family culture to bridge the generation gap and open their mind to communication with one another in a natural way. Now, going to no rae bang has become a normal part of life, and there have been good reviews of it. According to the review, no rae bang created a sound leisure culture.

Step 3 Traffic, Tourism and Shopping

1. Traffic

The flow of the traffic of Seoul is not out of the ordinary. About 10 million Seoulites are releasing a lot of heat for 24 hours. Like other metropolitan countries, the traffic jam of Seoul is serious.

According to the National Statistical Office (2006), the average number of cars per household in South Korea is 0.86. This shows that every family has about one car. The Korean government has run 'The 10th-day-no-driving System' and built roads and subways, but is inadequate to absorb the increasing amount of traffic. Because the traffic is crawling at a snail's pace at rush hour, people are again interested in public transportation.

Subway is the most preferred public transportation. The subway enables passengers to be on time because it is not only safe but its service time is also kept correctly. It boasts a clean facility with heating and cooling. Because in Seoul nine subway lines are in operation, subways are the most important means of transportation for Seoulites and the residents around Seoul. Also, subway lines run in cities such as Busan, Daegu and Incheon.

There is subway tour for people who want to travel about anywhere in Seoul. The whole family can enjoy the holiday at Lotte World and the Lotte World Folk Museum if they get off the subway at Jamsil Station on Line 2.

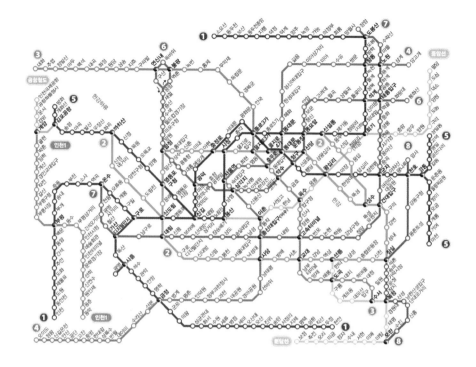

You can visit the Pulmuone Kimchi Museum if you get off the subway at Samseong Station on Line 2. You can easily go to Gyeongbok Palace if you get on the subway at any station on Line 3. Also transferring stations, shopping malls and music and dance performances are done and can enjoy subway culture and a comfortable place of meeting. Information of subways can be obtained on the internet, you can check how long it takes to get to the destination and information of events and performances before leaving home.

The traffic of Seoul looks complicated, but the system of it is well constructed. Transportation cards started to be supplied in 1996, and so there is no need to carry around change. The card is used when passengers transfer the subway to bus. The transfer fee varies according to the number of transfers and the distance, but the basic fare is free. If you use a transportation card, you get a 100 won discount from the regular cash payment. The cash amount on the card can be recharged and used again.

There are train lines in each area including the Gyeongbu Line which links Seoul and Busan. It takes roughly 6 hours by car to get from Seoul to Busan. But, the Korean Train Express (KTX) is so fast that it only takes 3 hours. You can reserve tickets on the website of the Korea Railroad Corporation (KORAIL) (http://www.korail.go.kr). An express bus can take you comfortably to the countryside. You can go and return somewhere in time because exclusive bus lanes are commenced on weekends. Tickets can be reserved on the website of the Seoul Express Bus Terminal (SEBUT) (http://www.exterminal.co.kr). There are domestic flights in Seoul and other large cities such as Jeju, Busan, Gwangju, Sokcho, Cheongju, and Ulsan. South Korea has two major airlines Korean Airlines (KAL) and Asiana Airlines.

2. Tourism and shopping

Famous tourist attractions

If you want to see the whole view of Seoul, you can see it at the top of the 63 Building in Yeuido or the Seoul Tower on Mount Nam. If you visit the Namsan Hanok Village on the way from the Seoul Tower, you can experience traditional Korean housing lifestyle, eat traditional Korean foods and watch performances.

If you go to the Korean Folk Village is located in Yongin near Seoul, you can experience Korean ancestors' lifestyle. The following amusement parks have a lot of exciting rides to relieve your stress in one go: Lotte World in

Amusement Park

Seoul, Seoul Land in Gwacheon, and Everland in Yongin. In Everland, called Korea's Disneyland, there are a lot of interesting things, such as four-season flower festivals, animal shows, and indoor and outdoor water parks for people of all ages.

If you plan on a long journey, visit scenic spots and places of historic interest, folk villages, Buddhist temples, hot springs and famous mountains designated as a national park in rural areas. Climbing is recommended because Korea especially has a beautiful nature harmonizing with mountains. If you follow the Baekdudaegan, which forms the backbone of the Korean Peninsula, there are large and small beautiful mountains, such as Mount Seorak in Gangwon-do, Mount Jiri in the south and Mount Halla in Jeju Island.

Because it snows a lot in Mount Seorak (1708m) in the winter, it is famous as sledge parks and ski resorts as well as climbing. Recently, Southeast Asian people come to this place to enjoy snow in the winter. Mount Jiri (1915m) is widely across Gyeongsang-do and Jeolla-do. Arts and literature have developed in Namwon, Jeollabuk-do because of the beauty of Mount Jiri. Namwon has produced many master singers of *pan so ri* 판소리 (traditional Korean narrative songs) and is the birthplace of the story of Chun-Hyang, a representative Korean beauty. Mount Halla (1950m) soars in the middle of Jeju Island and is the highest mountain in South Korea. It has a special geological structure due to volcanic activities and has a lovely pollution-free nature where the four seasons can bee seen.

Gyeongju is a good place for a trip to historic sites or Buddhist temples. The whole city of Gyeong-Ju-Si is a historic site of a history of thousand years. These days there is such a trip as 'Temple Stay' where people can experience the peaceful Buddhist temple lifestyle of Korea. The trip is popular among foreign tourists. If you belong to a new generation, it would be good to tour drama and movie filming sites related to the Korean Wave. If you are a woman, hot springs and beauty treatment courses would be good. You can obtain more information on the website of the Korea Tourism Organization (http://www.visitkorea.or.kr).

Regional Culture Festivals

These days, turing regional culture into tourist products has become trendy. Here is the list of traditional Korean festivals: (1) International Maskdance Festival in Andong, Gyeongsangbuk-do, (2) Insam Festival in Geumsan, Chungcheongnam-do, (3) Chunhyang Festival in Namwon, Jeollabuk-do, where the traditional beauty is shown off, (4) World Kimchi Culture Festival in Gwangju, Jeollannam-do, (5) Rice Cultural Festival in Icheon, Gyeonggi-do, (6) Ceramic Festival in Icheon, Gyeonggi-do, (7) Idong Rice Wine Festival in Pocheon, Gyeonggi-do, and (8) Idong Rib

Festival in Pocheon, Gyeonggi-do. Pocheon has many mountains and is famous for its delicious traditional Korean wine rice made of clean underground water from these mountains. If you drink with beef ribs cooked in charcoal fire, you can feel a sensational Korean taste. n addition, there are regional festivals with a long tradition, such as Hansan Victory Festival (October) in Tongyeong, Gyeongsangnam-do, Lamp Festival (April) in Jindo, Jeollanam-do, Naval Festival (March) in Jinhae, Gyeongsangnam-do, Dano Festival (June) in Gangneung, Gangwon-do, and Textile Festival in Daegu, Gyeongsangbuk-do. The regional cultural festivals have achieved a high level of satisfaction from visitors because these visitors do not only watch exhibitions and performances but they can also participate in many events.

Clothes Shopping Heaven

Korea is called 'Clothes Shopping Heaven.'

Thanks to the Seoul Olympics and international events, it has been globally known that Korean products are cheaper and better than foreign ones. South Korea's clothing fashion is especially popular. The most well known places among foreigners are Itaweon Market, Namdaemun Market and Dongdaemun Market, which are located in Seoul. There is no problem in English communication because Itaweon Market is a shopping district which was formed around the US armed forces. Here, you can buy all kinds of miscellaneous goods including accessories and clothes.

Namdaemun Market is the place visited by all foreigners touring Seoul. This market has everything, including imported goods and simple articles for daily use. It is especially well known that clothing products in the Namdaemun Market are cheapest in South Korea. When it becomes midnight, the market is crowded with traders of rural areas who come to the market to buy products. English housewives also buy things cheaply in

Shopping center

the market at dawn.

Recently 'Doosan Tower' and 'Migliore' in the Dongdaemun Market are popular as major clothing shopping malls for the new generation. This is because these malls have every fashionable items satisfying young people's tastes, arrange products so that customers can shop at one place and their items are relatively cheaper compared to department stores. Many students want to buy their fashionable items at least once. The Dongdaemun Market has a fun shopping atmosphere. For example, instant dance paties are opened by young people. People can shop conveniently because in the market there are also the Lotte Department Store, the Shinsaegae Department Store and many large shopping malls, such as E-Mart.

Traditional Markets

There are many types of special stores in Seoul. The Yongsan Electronic Shopping Center has good quality computers, mobile phones and a lot of types of electronic products. The center has a sale on its goods in the end of year, in the new year, during the admission period and in the vacation season. The Garak Market, located in Seoul, is the market to sell agricultural and marine products produced in the whole area of South Korea. The Noryagjin Fish Market is a nation-wide trading center for marine products in South Korea. The Dongdaemun Gyeongdong Market is famous for medicine herbs.

The Insa-dong Market and the Whanghak-dong Market are the places to experience Korea's native folklore, institutions and customs. The Insa-dong Market is famous for the street of traditional Korean arts and picked as a tourist route by many foreign tourists. In this market, Korea's cultural products can be appreciated quickly and street performances, such as *pan so ri* 판소리 (traditional Korean narrative songs) and *pung mul no ri* 풍물놀이 (farmer's musical play) are sometimes done. The Whanghak-dong Market is an antique market and called 'Flea Market.' This marketplace is a typical flea market to sell old or second hand articles made in foreign countries as well as Korea. The Whanghak-dong Market is located in the Chunggye Creek. If you go there, you can experience Korean people's past poverty and ordinary Korean people's taste for arts. Also. if you go to a traditional market in the countryside, you can still feel the old atmosphere of Korean rural areas deeply.

Websites related to 'Korean culture and tourism'

1. Gateway to Korea (http://korea.net)

2. Hi Korea, E-Government for Foreigners (http://www.hikorea.go.kr)

3. The Ministry of Culture, Sports, and Tourism (http://www.mct.go.kr)

4. The Seoul Metropolitan Government (http://www.seoul.go.kr)

5. Korea Tourism Organization (http://www.visitkorea.or.kr)

6. Center for International Affairs (http://www.ikorea.ac.kr)

7. What's On Communications, Korean Tourism Culture (http://www.whatsonkorea.com)

8. Life in Korea, Introduction to Korean Travel and Culture (http://lifeinkorea.com)

9. Overseas Koreans Foundation, Get to Know about Korea (http://pr.korean.net)

10. Cultural Heritage Administration of Korea (http://www.cha.go.kr)

Exercises

01 Read the following examples and if right put a O inside the (   ) and
   if wrong put a X instead.
   1) Taekwondo is one of the representative national sports in Korea. (   )
   2) Takewondo rookies train, wearing the black belt. (   )
   3) In the 2002 FIFA World Cup, the Korean team created the legend of
      advancing to the semifinals. (   )
   4) The mysterious efficacy of in sam is scientifically proved today. (   )
   5) Judo was a folk sport taking place in a ring of sand, and the winer was
      called '*jang sa* 장사 (the strongest man).' (   )

02 These days there is a trip where people can experience the peaceful
   Buddhist temple lifestyle of Korea. The trip is popular among foreign
   tourists. What is this tour program called?

03 Explain about the traffic system showing the statement that the traffic
   of Seoul looks complicated, but the system of it is well constructed.

04 Give an example of Korean people's cheering heat in the 2002 FIFA
   World Cup Korea/Japan which was without parallel in the world
   history of soccer.

05 Explain why Koreans especially like hiking. Also compare Korean
   people's leisure culture and that of your country and discuss with
   others about the comparison.

Chapter

12

Lunar New Year's Day, gift money, be happy!

Step 1 Korean Festive Days

1. Lunar New Year's Day

Se Bae and Cha Rey Sang

The festive days that Koreans consider to be biggest is Lunar New Year's Day and Harvest Moon Festival.

Since old times, Korea people believed that they can enjoy good harvest and prosperity because of the protection of the absolute being in the heaven and their ancestral spirits. Korean festive days and seasonal customs came form Korean people's rituals of thanking the protection. The order of traditional Korean holidays follows the 24 seasonal divisions.

Lunar New Year's Day is the 1st day of the year by the lunar calender.

This day has a great significance for Korean people because they make New Year's calls on the heaven and their ancestors to pray good harvest and prosperity and make a fresh start in the new year. On the last day of December, that is, on the previous day of Lunar New Year's Day, Korean people cleaned their houses, washed their bodies and prepared for meeting the new year. In the night of the previous day, they lit up their houses to block the bad luck of the darkness and to receive good luck. Also, they stayed up for the new year. On the previous day, children tried hard not to go to sleep because it was said that if people go to sleep in the night of the

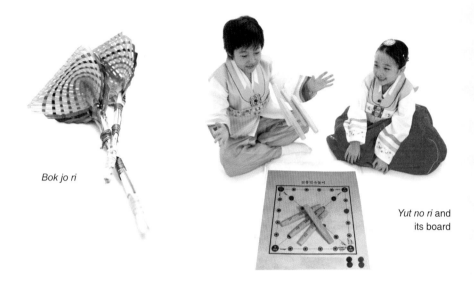

Bok jo ri

Yut no ri and
its board

Kite flying

Je gi cha gi

last day of December their eyebrows turn white. When they see someone sleeping in the night, they painted the person's eyebrows white and made fun of him or her in the morning of the new year.

In the morning of Lunar New Year's Day, Korean people hold *cha rey* 차례 (ancestral rites) to honor and give thanks to their ancestors and then they eat the foods laid on the *cha rey sang* 차례상 (ancestral rite table) with their family. The main dish of Lunar New Year's Day is *tteok guk* 떡국 (rice-cake soups).

Especially on this day, children wear '*seol bim* 설빔 (Lunar New Year's garment)' and make '*se bae* 세배 (Lunar New Year's formal bows)' to older members of their family. When performing *se bae*, they say, 'Happy New Year!' After receiving se bae, the older members say, 'May the hopes of the new year come to pass.' The saying is called '*deok dam* 덕담 (word of blessing).' Children are served light refreshments or gives '*se baet don* 세뱃돈 (gifts of money)' after making their bows. Because newly minted money is used as *se baet don*, people go to a bank to change their bills into the cleanest ones in the bank so as to prepare for *se baet don*. Lunar New Year's Day is a very exciting holiday for Korean children because of *se baet don*, good foods and beautiful seol bim.

In the morning of Lunar New Year's Day, new strainers were brought and hung up in the house with red string to bring good luck to the home in the coming year. These new strainers were called '*bok jo ri* 복조리', a compound word of '*bok* 복 (good fortune)' and '*jori* 조리 (strainer).' *Jo ri* was used to separate rice from the stones when rice being washed. The word *bok jo ri* was derived from the concave part of *jo ri* which means cultivating good fortune. So, Korean people hung up *bok jo ri* in the house on Lunar New Year's Day, hoping for letting a lot of fortunes be cultivated.

Entertainment culture of Lunar New Year's Day

Korean people enjoyed many traditional Korean sports in the afternoon after finishing performing se bae. Boys flew kites in the sky or kicked *je gi* 제기 (a shuttle cock made by wrapping paper around an old brass coin with a hole in the center and inserting feathers through the hole). Korean people usually flew kites in the windy winter. Korean kites are smaller and stronger than Western ones. The typical Korean kite is a rectangular one with the *tae geuk* (태극) (pattern consisting of a circle with two interlocking comma shapes), which is called *bang pae yeon* 방패연 (a shield kite). Girls played *neol ttwi gi* 널뛰기 (Korean seasawing). Two girls stood at each end and jump in turn, sending the girl in the other end flying up into the air. A long time ago, women were not allowed to go out without the permission of their parents. When playing *neol ttwi gi*, they could see a neighborhood man over the wall.

Adults usually played *yut* 윷 (game played with four sticks) on Lunar New Year's Day. Because yut was played by two teams, it gave a pleasure to people. Players used *yut pan* 윷판 (a board marked with a crossed circle), five markers per team, and four sticks, each rounded on one side and flat on the other. The sticks were thrown into the air, and the number of sticks falling with flat side up determined the number of spaces the marker could move forward. The moves were named after five animals: (1) one stick falling flat side up is *do* 도 (1 point), meaning pig, (2) two sticks is *gae* 개 (2 points), meaning dog, (3) three sticks is *geol* 걸 (3 points), meaning ship, (4) four sticks is *yut* (4 points), meaning cow, and (5) all sticks round side up is *mo* 모 (5 points), meaning horse. When playing *yut*, players talked with their team members about putting the markers. Before throwing the sticks into the air, they cast a spell on the sticks, saying 'Come out, *mo!*' They cheered and clapped when all sticks were round side up. These days, people can learn yut on the internet.

However, today's Lunar New Year's Day is different from the past.

Hwa tu (flower cards)

Because South Korea is not an agricultural country, Korean people cannot enjoy traditional Korean sports together. These days, traditional Korean holidays give a great significance to Korean people because the family members get together and take a rest at the holidays. When the holidays come, the family members watch TV at home or become closer with one another playing *hwa tu* 화투 (flower cards).

Hwa tu is a card game which is widely used for amusement in South Korea. The deck of hwa tu consists of 48 cards. The 12 suits of it represent the 12 month of year, with each suit made up of 4 cards bearing pictures of flowers that bloom in that month: (1) pine in January, (2) plum blossom in February, (3) cherry blossom in March, (4) wisteria in April, (5) iris in May, (6) peony in June, (7) bush clover in July, (9) Susuki grass in August, (9) chrysanthemum in September, (10) maple in October, (11) willow in November, and (12) paulownia in December. Young people enjoy playing go-stop, a type of *hwa tu*. People must be careful of its addiction because the go-stop game can be a gambling if they play it excessively.

Korean men enjoy a silent holiday playing *ba duk* 바둑 (board game) or *jang gi* 장기 (Korean chess). Korean chess is shown in the movie 'Once Upon A Time In The Battlefield (2003).' In the movie there is a scene where the main characters play Korean chess and read the strategy of the other player. The scene shows well the characteristics of Korean chess. Ba duk is a board game which is played on a square board marked with 19 vertical and horizontal lines, making 361 intersection points called *jip* 집 (house). Players sit opposite each other and in turn place small round markers, one side white and the other black, on any vacant point on the board. Ba duk is widely spread throughout East Asian countries including South Korea, China and Japan, and it can be called the representative board game of the East. Korean players show high level of skills in international matches of ba duk.

Together with their family members, Korean people go to a thermal spring or *jjim jil bang* 찜질방 (Korean dry sauna) to wash away the fatigue of Lunar New Year's holidays. Families with many children enjoy the holidays by playing traditional Korean sports in tourist attractions, such as amusement parks and folk villages.

Neol ttwi gi (Korean jumping game)

2. *Jeong wol dae bo rum and dan o*

When Korea was an agricultural country, the mood of Lunar New Year's Day lasted to *jeong wol dae bo rum* 정월대보름 (First Full Moon Day) of the year. The 15th day of

Swing

the first lunar month called Jeong wol dae bo rum was a day when people made wishes looking at the full moon.

The morning of *jeong wol dae bo rum* was started by biting *bu reom* 부럼. The word *bu reom* refers to a collection of various kinds of nuts, such as pine nuts, chestnuts, peanuts and walnuts. Korean people believed that people can stay healthy because the body is not covered in boils if they bites bu reom.

O gok bap 오곡밥 (five-grain rice) and *na mul* 나물 (seasoned greens and vegetables) were served on the morning table on *jeong wol dae bo rum*. Generally, the five grains are rice, millet, red beans, sorghum and black beans. Korean people dried green vegetables in the autumn. They parboiled these dried vegetables in hot water and seasoned with various ingredients to make *na mul*. *Na mul* had a great significance because *na mul* gave the vitamins they needed in the winter. Together with their family members, Korean people drunk a cup of wine called '*gwi bal gi sul* 귀밝이술' on the morning of the full moon day. Children drunk it because it was said that if people drink *gwi bal gi sul* they can clear the ears and make them ready to hear good news.

Dan o is the fifth day of the fifth lunar month of the year. On this day, women washed their hair with *chang po mul* 창포물 (water infused with sweet flags). It was said that people will have thick lustrous hair if they wash their hair chang po mul. Men played *ssi reum* 씨름 (Korean wrestling) in a ring of sand, and women performed *geu ne ta gi* 그네타기 (swinging). It was said that when women played on the swings on dan o, they washed away their stress looking towards the wide world. While looking at women swinging high towards the sky, some people said that the sight was like a taoist fairy going up to the heaven. There is also a custom of giving gifts of folding fans to prepare for the coming summer.

Gang gang sul lae

3. Harvest Moon Festival

Chu seok 추석 (Harvest Moon Festival) is the 15th of August by the lunar calendar and is called '*han ga wi* 한가위.' Together with *seol* 설 (Lunar New Year's Day), Harvest Moon Festival is the biggest festive day in Korea. *Chu seok* was a day for thanking the ancestors for good harvest. On the morning of *chu seok*, the family gathered at the home of the oldest male to hold ancestral rites. *Chu seok* has a similar meaning to Thanksgiving Day in US. Korean people set plenty of *haet gok sik* 햇곡식 (newly harvest grains), fruits, *song pyeon* 송편 (half-moon shaped rice cake) and offering wine on the ritual table. Song pyeon and offering wine were made of *haep ssal* 햅쌀 (newly harvested rice). On *chu seok*, Korean people specially eat *song pyeon* among all the rice cakes. The mood of *chu seok* is shown well by the sight of the whole family sitting together and making *song pyeon*.

There are many customs of *chu seok*, such as *nong ak* 농악 (farmer's music), *jul da ri gi* 줄다리기 (tug of war) and *gang gang sul lae* 강강술래 (circle dance for women). It is a game where two teams pull opposite ends of rope in an attempt to drag the opposition over a central line. Neighboring villages competed to show their power of unity through *jul da ri gi*. These days, jul da ri gi is performed in many school sports festivals. The tug of war strengthens a sense of community and fellowship because people should pull the rope with one voice to win the game. *Gang gang sul lae* is a dance where under the bright moonlight, groups of well-dressed women form a circle and start moving very slowly clockwise and then counterclockwise around a solo singer who dances in the center. The origin of the dance goes back to Admiral Sun-Sin Lee (1545-1598). During the Japanese invasion of 1592, Admiral Lee gathered the women in Jindo, Jeollanam-do, to the seashore under the moonlight and ordered them to dance so as to make the Japanese invaders believe that there were many Korean soldiers guarding the seashore. The woman in the center sings the lyrics, while the other women sing the refrain, '*gang gang sul lae* 강강술래 (watch the surrounds).'

There are so many people who visit their hometowns on Lunar New Year's Day and Harvest Moon Festival that the phrase '*min jok dae i dong* 민족대이동 (a mass exodus of Korean people)' was created to describe it. The people who do not go to their hometown on Korean festive days repent of it and call themselves '*bul hyo ja* 불효자 (an dutiful son or daughter).' Because the roads to the hometowns are packed with cars all at once, South Korea's roads become heavily congested. Usually it takes 4 hours to get from Seoul to Daegu, but on the holidays there are times when it takes over 15 hours. These holidays are short and just lasts 4 days.

Further, the roads are filled with traffic jams. Nonetheless, Korean people get the sufficient amount of energy to recover and then return to work. When they return, their bundles are filled with clusters of foods from their parents. These holiday customs show the characteristics of Korean families. So to speak, Korean people realize a place in their heart because Korean festive days confirm that they have close links with their family members even if they live in a society with material civilization.

4. Winter solstice

Red bean porridge

The winter solstice is the longest night of the year. This day is between *dae seol* 대설 (time of heavy snow) and *so han* 소한 (little cold) according to the 24 seasonal divisions. Generally, the winter solstice falls on December by the solar calendar. On this day, Korean people ate *pat juk* 팥죽 (thick red bean porridge with small round rice cakes), and sprinkled the porridge around the house and large trees nearby. They believed that the red color of it wards off evil spirits. The small round rice cakes are made of glutinous rice flour. The number of these cakes is decided by the age of the person who eats it. So, people say that if someone eats pat juk, he or she grows a year older. On this day, peple cook enough pat juk to share with the neighbors.

Step 2 Religion

1. Folk beliefs

Along time ago Korean people believed that every object in the natural world has a spirit.

They performed rituals to spirits indwelling in objects, such as big trees, mountains and stones, in the nature to escape from the misfortune which cannot be warded off by their power. They feared the sky because they believed that the sky is the best of all objects of worship in the nature. They did rituals towards the sky to pray for good harvest and their family's prosperity. Taoism and geomancy came from the principal that man is one of objects and should live in harmony with the laws of nature. Both of them can be ideas of the order of nature rather than religions. Taoism is a philosophical system based on the principal. Geomancy is a method to locate propitious sites for the living and graves for the dead. These kinds of ideas have been driving forces in Korean people's improving their religion because these ideas were never in conflict with other religions when they were introduced into Korea.

Jang seung (Korean
traditional totem pole)

It can be said that shamanism is based on the order of
nature. In shamanism, *mu dang* 무당 (shaman) prays for
good fortunes as an intermediary between the spirits and
human beings. *Jang seung* 장승 (Korean totem poles)
derived from worship of the phallus or from towering
spirit posts and menhirs and put up at the entrance to a
village to guard the village against evil spirits. There was
the faith of sam *sin hal meo ni* 삼신할머니 (the Birth
Grandmother), a goddess thought to oversee the birth of
babies and the well-being of a child. *Jeom* 점 (fortune-
telling) was popular in the past. Korean people consulted
fortune-tellers about their future. They also consulted
fortune-tellers on important matters in life, such as *gung
hap* 궁합 (martial harmony between a man and woman)
and choosing days for weddings. Also when the new year
comes, people check the fortune of the year according to

the book '*to jeong bi gyeol* 토정비결', written by Ji-Han Lee (1517-1578). This book tells the fortune of a person based on their precise moment of birth. These days many people check their fortune according to the book on the internet or consult internet fortune-tellers on their fortune. Young people check their fortune half from belief and half for fun.

2. Confucianism, Buddhism and Taoism

Confucianism, Buddhism, and Taoism came early into Korea and became its major religions. Buddhism was introduced into Korea in A.D. 374 during the period of Goguryeo. Buddhism grew until it adopted as the state religion by Silla and Goryeo and became people's values and visions of the universe in those days. Buddhism is base on mercy. According to Buddhism, all actions are repaid and nirvana is eventually achieved if good deeds are done. Confucianism was an ethical and philosophical system developed from the teachings of the Chinese philosopher Confucius. Confucianism was made a religion by Seong-Gye Lee, who found Joseon in 1392, so as to unite the people mentally. Confucianism aims to inspire and preserve the good management of family and society, based on the four ethical percepts benevolent lover, righteousness, decorum and wise leadership. Taoism aims to every factitious thing and live in harmony with the laws of nature.

Catholicism first came to Korea as Wester scholarly pursuit other than as a religion in the late Joseon period. *Cheon do gyo* 천도교 (the Religion of the Heavenly Way) was founded by Je-U Choi (1824-1864) to oppose Western learning and religion, when Western powers came to Korea and then Western learning was started in Korea. The principle of *cheon do gyo* is '*in nae cheon* 인내천', which means that the man is identical with 'ha nul nim 하늘님 (the God of cheon do gyo).' *Cheon do gyo* proclaimed the equality of all human beings.

3. Modern people and religion

Foreigners visiting Seoul are amazed at the number of crosses hung on buildings. In Korea, Catholicism was introduced into Korea earlier than Protestantism. Catholicism is called the Roman Catholic Church. Catholicism came to Korea through China in 18th century during the late Joseon period. Because of the problem of ancestral rites, Catholicism was in conflict with a society of Joseon, ruled by Confucianism. So, Catholic fathers were prosecuted and martyred. Protestantism was introduced by American missionaries in the 20th century. In particular,

Cathedral and church

Protestant missionaries rendered medical service and education as a means of disseminating their credo and founded Protestant schools, such as Yonhui Junior College (now Yonsei University) and Ewha Woman's Junior College (now Ewha Womans University). The two Christian doctrines 'love of neighbor' and 'public spirit' have played key roles in Protestantism's rapid growth in South Korea in difficult times, such as Japan's occupation ot Korea and the Korean War.

The present distribution of religious population in South Korea is as follows: (1) Buddhism (23.3%), (2) Protestantism (19.7), (3) Catholicism (6.6%), (4) Confucianism (0.5% or less), (5) *cheon do gyo* (0.5% or less), and (6) Won Buddhism (0.5% or less). This shows that a sum of the number of Catholic and Protestant believers exceeds the number of Buddhists.

Recently, a variety of foreign religions have come to South Korea because there has been an increase in employees of foreign companies and their families who live in South Korea because of Korean economic growth. Korean people are very flexible towards religious rites of these foreigners. This is because Korean people have put stress on the values of the world of spirits since ancient times. Buddha's Birthday (Lunar April 8) and Christmas (December 25) were designated as public holidays in South Korea.

Exercises

01 Read the following sentences and put O in the (   ), if wrong put X instead.

  1) The most biggest festive days for Korean people are Lunar New Year's Day and Harvest Moon Festival. (   )

  2) Lunar New Year's Day is the 1st day of the year by the solar calender. On this day, people eat *haep ssal bap* 햅쌀밥 (cooked one from newly harvested rice) and *song pyeon* 송편 (half-moon shaped rice cake). (   )

  3) There are so many people who visit their hometowns on Lunar New Year's Day and Harvest Moon Festival that the phrase '*min jok dae i dong* 민족대이동 (a mass exodus of Korean people)' was created to describe it. (   )

  4) Korean people eat *pat juk* 팥죽 (thick red bean porridge with small round rice cakes) on the winter solstice. People say that if someone eats *pat juk*, he or she grows a year older. (   )

  5) If children make '*se bae* 세배 (Lunar New Year's formal bows)' to older members of their family on Lunar New Year's Day, the older members give '*deok dam* 덕담 (word of blessing)' and delicious foods. (   )

02 It is a day when people made wishes looking at the full moon. They ate *o gok bap* 오곡밥 (five-grain rice) and *na mul* 나물 (seasoned greens and vegetables) and drunk a cup of wine called '*gwi bal gi sul* 귀밝이술' on the morning of the day. What is the name of the festive day?

03 The following examples show traditional Korean sports or customs. Divide the examples into the one which are played usually by men into Category A and the ones which are played usually by women into

Category B.

| Examples | *gang gang sul lae* 강강술래, *yut* 윷, *neol ttwi gi* 널뛰기, *hwa tu* 화투, *ba duk* 바둑, *geu ne ta gi* 그네타기 |

04 Explain customs of folk religions in Korean people's lifestyle, together with their example.

05 Many religions coexist in the current korean society. State all the religion holidays you know.